LEARNING TO LIVE ALONE

LEARNING TO LIVE ALONE

◆

A HANDBOOK FOR WIDOWERS

Bob Hurmence

iUniverse, Inc.
New York Lincoln Shanghai

LEARNING TO LIVE ALONE
A HANDBOOK FOR WIDOWERS

Copyright © 2007 by Bob Hurmence

All rights reserved. No part of this book may be used or reproduced by any means, graphic, electronic, or mechanical, including photocopying, recording, taping or by any information storage retrieval system without the written permission of the publisher except in the case of brief quotations embodied in critical articles and reviews.

iUniverse books may be ordered through booksellers or by contacting:

iUniverse
2021 Pine Lake Road, Suite 100
Lincoln, NE 68512
www.iuniverse.com
1-800-Authors (1-800-288-4677)

Because of the dynamic nature of the Internet, any Web addresses or links contained in this book may have changed since publication and may no longer be valid.

The views expressed in this work are solely those of the author and do not necessarily reflect the views of the publisher, and the publisher hereby disclaims any responsibility for them.

ISBN: 978-0-595-44254-6 (pbk)
ISBN: 978-0-595-88585-5 (ebk)

Printed in the United States of America

Contents

Introduction vii

Part I Suddenly Single 1
CHAPTER 1 The Sting of Death 3
CHAPTER 2 Why Me? 8
CHAPTER 3 Help From Family and Friends 13

Part II What Am I Going To Do? 19
CHAPTER 4 When Everybody's Gone Home 21
CHAPTER 5 Stuff—Keep It or Lose It 28
CHAPTER 6 Take A Skills Inventory 36
CHAPTER 7 Free at Last? 39
CHAPTER 8 Polishing the Silver 41

Part III The Time Consuming Business of Eating 47
CHAPTER 9   You Can't Eat at McDonald's Everyday 49
CHAPTER 10 The Tools of the Cooking Trade 53
CHAPTER 11 A New Look at the Supermarket 57
CHAPTER 12 Stocking the Pantry 62
CHAPTER 13 Boiling An Egg and Beyond 64
CHAPTER 14 What's for Supper? 72

Part IV *Making Adjustments*.................. *81*

Chapter 15 Teaching Time To Fly...................... 83

Chapter 16 Is There Anyone Up There?................. 88

Chapter 17 Tomorrow and Tomorrow and Tomorrow 91

About the Author 93

Introduction

My wife's name was Boots. Although she shared her maiden name with me I was instructed never to use it unless it was required on some legal document. Boots is a great name for a Texas girl. Far from being "country" Boots loved life, her children, her friends, her God and me. I returned that love as best I could. She was beautiful, strict but loving with her children, endowed with a great sense of humor, a Republican and a marvelous kisser. I miss her terribly.

This book is not about Boots although you will get to know a little about her if you choose to read what I have written. This manuscript is about my experiences as I adjust to living by myself. Writing it was therapy and a partial healing of the hole my wife's loss has left in my life. If you are enduring under this same condition some of what is happening to me will have happened to you as well. Some of my advice will be old stuff but, hopefully you will get an idea or two that will help for the unique condition that becoming a widower entails. Even some widows who have read its content claim to have received some benefit as a result.

I have tried to furnish practical advice on the basic adjustments a man that has been married for most of his life must make. You will find only a part of yourself here for we are all unique with somewhat different problems and skills. It is my hope that reading this book will help you as much as writing it has helped me.

My wife passed away suddenly and unexpectedly. It left me devastated, alone, and totally unprepared for the life I was to live. I'm making adjustments, learning to live alone, to do housework, to cook, to clean, to launder, to remember birthdays, to write thank you notes, to call the plumber, to keep my clothes cleaned and pressed, to keep my house and all of the thousand other things my wife took care of and which, for the most part I never gave a thought. I have been forced to change from just the man of the house to the woman of the house as well.

I'm better prepared for this obligation than most men I know. I have always been a pretty good cook and I have learned a few things about domestic chores during short-term illnesses my wife suffered over the years. My generation of husbands were almost exclusively the breadwinners. Our wives did not work outside the home unless it was absolutely necessary or it was their desire to do so. I earned our living and my wife took care of the household. As a result I never sewed on a button, ironed a shirt, washed my clothes, or cooked a complete meal.

This arrangement is rare today. All of my children, like all of the younger married couples I know, are joint wage earners. This is brought about by the economic necessities our way of life now demands of us. It's a lucky woman today who can afford the luxury of being a stay-at-home mom. Sharing the wage earning responsibilities has required most men to share some of the domestic duties with his wife. I say some of the duties because it is generally true that women get the heavier load at home and much of the help they do receive is half hearted at best. Do you know a man who can dust with enthusiasm? So while the modern male is better prepared to care for himself than men of my generation, he is woefully naïve about what he will face, if, for some incomprehensible reason, he is, as I now find myself, suddenly single.

Assuming the duties a husband performs in a marriage is no less daunting to a woman who is left behind. She now must balance the checkbook, take out the garbage, check the circuit breaker, change the light bulbs, sharpen the knives, tighten the screws, loosen the bolts, oil the hinges, unstick the stuck, open the jar, climb the ladder, and maintain the car. Lord knows what else she will be called upon to perform. I do not want to demean for one moment the challenges of widowhood but I only feel qualified to deal here with what I, and other widowers must face. The brutal fact is that both genders confronted by the death of their spouse must now assume roles that are both new and sometimes difficult if not impossible to perform. A number of movies have been made over the years depicting the dilemmas faced when mothers switch places with their daughters and men switch places with women. They are all presented as comedies. Assuming the role of your spouse is not a comedy.

Many years ago I read a book by Phillip Wylie titled, *The Disappearance*. The plot of the book depicted what would happen when all of the women on earth suddenly disappeared and in alternate chapters what would happen if all of the men on earth suddenly disappeared. It is somewhat outdated today because the problems faced by each sex were influenced by the mores and prejudices of the times. Still, what the widow and widower of today must face can be likened to a similar but more personal fate. It may not be world wide, but it is wide enough to encompass the world of those who are left behind.

So, this book's purpose is to help any widower cope with everyday life in a world that is generally built for two. It may also help the children of a parent to understand what their dad, brother, or uncle living the single life once again is experiencing. It is my hope that through reading about my experiences as a widower, a fellow traveler will gain a deeper insight into his own dilemma and thereby better cope with his own experiences in living alone.

I have been left alone after forty-two years of marriage and I'm learning how to cope with that fact. The single life is doable as I am discovering day by day. Both long and short-term widowers whom I have talked with seem to face more unfamiliar challenges than their feminine counterparts and I hope through sharing my experiences, this book will be of some help along the way.

PART I
Suddenly Single

1

The Sting of Death

Like most men I planned to be the first to die and thereby leave all of the problems to my wife. She had always said she wanted to die first because she did not want to become a part of one of those groups of elderly ladies sitting in a restaurant accompanied by one male survivor. I could sympathize with that because I certainly did not want to be the one male survivor of my wife's potential widows.

In anticipating my earlier demise, I, at least, approached this possibility with basic planning. I was professional about it. I had made a will, itemized the insurance policies, listed the names and phone numbers of our accountant, our banker, our lawyer, and out investment broker. My wife was signatory on all of our accounts and I had kept our bank account balanced and solvent. Fortunately we had little debt. The house and cars were paid for and our credit cards were paid up each month. There were no installment payments. Few people today have this luxury. We are not wealthy by American standards but we were certainly better off than the majority of people in this world.

We had even purchased a burial policy some twenty years ago and paid it off over a seven-year period. When we tried to tell the children about this policy they did not want to hear about it, nor did they ever want to contemplate the possibility of our deaths. But we did. My wife was very adamant about what to do if she should die. She did not want an open casket nor did she want me or any of our children or relatives to view her body once she died. I believe the same way and I honored her request. As a result of the prepayment, much of what was called for following her death was eased considerably. Many do not have this ease of mind and I urge those of you who can afford it to examine the possibility of making such a purchase. You do not need the agony of shopping for a funeral in the midst of your grief if you can possibly avoid it.

On the morning my wife died I got up first but not by more than a few minutes. We wake early, around five thirty. I let our dog, Chester, out by way of our back door. There is a dog door available and in regular use with the one exception of this morning ritual. I suppose it is our canine's way of exerting his authority over me at a time when my resistance is low. When I returned to the bedroom my wife was sitting on the edge of the bed and said she was having difficulty breathing. Knowing such complaints might indicate a heart attack, I asked if she wanted me to call 911. She said, "No," But in another minute, she had changed her mind and asked me to call. I explained my wife's symptoms to the operator who sent an ambulance but advised to have my wife breathe deeply through her nose. I know she tried this but to no avail. Prior to the arrival of the ambulance, I got out a fresh nightgown at my wife's request and I helped her change. How bad could it be, I thought, if she wanted to change gowns before going to the emergency room. She was almost recovered from extensive foot surgery but still wore a removable cast. The cast restricted her movements considerably and she could not do much more than stand with the help of a walker. It would be impossible for her to walk down the hall.

The EMS crew tried to put an oxygen mask on her but she kept removing it in an futile attempt to get some air. All this time I was doing my best to help get the gurney back to the bedroom. It was too big and our hallway was too narrow to make the turn. I immediately got a wheelchair we had been using and wheeled my wife into the living room so she could get on the gurney. By the time she had been placed in the ambulance I had thrown on some clothes and was ready to follow it to the hospital. I spent all this time while running and fetching, making arrangements to go to the hospital. All of this activity (putting on clothes, securing the dog and the house) denied me the opportunity to help with my wife. So much was going on around her that I never had an opportunity to talk to her, to reassure her or to tell her that I loved her. I shall regret this to my dying day. Why couldn't I have held her hand, given her a kiss, or told her I love her? It all happened so fast.

We live no more than three or four miles from the hospital and the road we took was almost all major thoroughfare. I followed the ambulance but by the time I had found a parking place and entered the emergency room they had placed her in a room with four or five people hovering over her. They would not let me enter and escorted me to a waiting area, which, at 6:00 a.m., was virtually empty. A doctor did come by to assure me that they were tending to my wife and they suspected a blockage of some sort. I guess that is what he said, I really don't remember. I got the impression it was serious but up to that time I believed that if you got to the hospital everything would be all right. It wasn't.

The emergency room was empty, dimly lit and foreboding. I sat there with everything and nothing going through my mind. My wife was just fine last night.

She was looking forward to getting out of the cast and being able to put some weight on her foot. She had been hopping around for the last six weeks dependent on me to move her by wheelchair. Her confinement had made her irritable and she took her frustrations out on me. I understood why, but it did not make living together any easier. Now I wondered what this lung blockage thing would do to her recovery. I did not have long to wait. No more than thirty minutes from my arrival, a nurse came out to me and told me that my wife had died of a pulmonary embolism. Died? A pulmonary embolism? What was that? The shock was just beginning. In an effort to give me some consolation, the nurse said that she knew my wife was loved because there was not a line in her face. These words, the only ones I truly remember hearing that morning, have been etched in my memory.

I cannot erase that hospital experience from my mind. It returns at the oddest times, less painful now but no less clear. The doctor and the nurse were present with me in the waiting room. They explained how a blood clot had broken free and passed through the heart and lodged in the junction where the blood goes to both lungs—she suffocated. God, I hate to know that. I wonder if she knew she was dying. She had to think it. We all want to die in our sleep without suffering. I suppose if you have to die while you are otherwise healthy, suffocation or drowning is as easy a death as there is. But this is small consolation.

A sudden, unanticipated death is devastating. In such a short time your life has seemingly come to an end. What are you to do? Who are you to call? How did this happen? Why did this happen? Did you just ask me if you could harvest her organs? What funeral home do you want us to call? May I see her?

I'm certain there was an interval of time that passed but it has since become such a muddled mess of memory and emotion that I will never get the sequence of events in their proper order. When the nurse asked if I would permit the harvesting of organs I became numb. We had never discussed this and the question asked immediately was such a shock that a rational response was impossible. I said no. Next, I was asked about a funeral home. I couldn't think straight. I named the best known funeral home in the city but also mentioned that we had a prepaid burial policy. It didn't dawn on me at the time that this policy also covered mortuary services. As a result, I had to pay this funeral home over a thousand dollars for services included in my burial policy that I did not need had I only the presence of mind to call the cemetery. Evidently the nurse did not know how to advise me either.

Sudden death evokes such a jumble of emotions and hasty decisions, that there is not a way to be prepared for such a traumatic experience. Fortunately, your friends and then your children will ease you into the decisions that must be made. Call a friend as soon as you can. Call a friend even before you call your children. You need rational help and someone who can think straight. Take time to cry, pray, remember—but not too much. There is a great deal to do and grieving must come later. Arrangements must be made. You will be asked all too quickly about a funeral home, not for the funeral but for someplace to transfer the body. Other questions must be asked and answered in the case of accidental death. An autopsy must be performed. Be prepared for the organ-harvesting question. It's not one for which many of us are prepared. How heartless can they be? Can't this wait?

Death following an extended illness is no less painful. It is true that in such instances a lot of decisions in anticipation of death have probably been made, but the loss of a loved one is never easy. Your own personal agony in watching the love of your life die a sometimes painful but welcomed death can make a wound that will never fully heal. Well meaning friends can tell you that such a death is a blessing and, perhaps, it was for the deceased but it is no blessing to the survivor. I lost a sister to cancer many years ago and to this day I cannot forget holding her hand as excruciating pains sent spasms through her fragile body.

Funeral plans must be made. I cannot imagine a funeral without a church but I am sure it can be arranged. A church, your pastor, your Sunday school class, all will now be the rock you will stand on. The funeral home will know what else is required. Hopefully, you will not be alone in dealing with these issues: the casket, the cemetery, the burial plot, the day, the time, the church sanctuary the church chapel or a graveside service. Other things to consider are the reception, open or closed casket, regular or memorial service, cremation, the music, a soloist, a meal, the flowers, memorial options, the obituary and notification to family and friends.

If you do not have a church affiliation and your beliefs are such that a religious service or setting is not appropriate, you will still find the need for a memorial service of some sort. Friends and children will want to participate and funeral homes can provide help and a location for a tribute to the person you loved that fulfills your wishes.

Any service, religious or otherwise, is ultimately a celebration of the life of your wife. It is one of the many quirks of the English language that the word celebration is used in this instance. Memorial is perhaps a better term but any memory of your life together rejoices the feelings you experienced at the time and, as such, is a celebration.

Someone other than you must take charge to see that everyone is notified. That person will not know everyone. You must tell them whom of your family and relatives from out of town are to be notified. Fortunately my wife kept a complete and up to date address book which I relied upon with gratitude. I kept no such book. Had she not been so well organized, it would have been an ordeal and an unwelcome struggle to try to remember who should be notified. If you have no such book, I urge you to compile one and keep it current. If you are computer literate you may have compiled such a list on your computer and your computer can be a marvelous way of notifying a number of people with one common message.

Food will be arriving and you will need help in receiving and cataloging it. Plates will have to be returned and thank you cards written, so it is essential to keep good records. Friends will do this service except for the acknowledgements. That will be up to you. An obituary should be written. Help here is essential. Generally, you are in no position to do anything but edit such a document.

To begin with, a grown child, a brother-in-law, a sister or a combination of people who knew your spouse should write the original draft. The newspaper is full of samples. It will be your responsibility to edit and give final approval to this tribute. Generally a photo is to be included and it would be helpful if you have a suitable picture in your computer that can be properly cropped and sized to fit the column requirements of the newspaper. A contemporary photograph is preferable.

A minister, if he is worth his salt, can, in the guise of preparing for the funeral service, lead you and your family down a memory lane that can be the kind of therapy you need at this time. In my own instance our pastor led the family through a time of recalling all of the loving and humorous days of our lives with my wife. We laughed. We cried. We shared feelings and we were somehow closer to each other and to their mother and my only true love than we had ever dared to be when she was alive. Friends will do this, too, as they express their sorrow and concern. It all helps—it does not cure.

You must be involved in everything and it's not fair. You want time to grieve, to mourn your loss, to say goodbye privately. That time will come but it won't really come until it's all over and everyone has gone back to their lives. Then there will be time to sit quietly and weep.

We have all experienced the death of people who have touched our lives. None is as personal as the loss of your life-long companion. I hope you have a faith to carry you through the sadness.

2
Why Me?

There are plenty of books and pamphlets on how to understand grief and some on how to deal with it. It is not a skill I want to learn. Time is supposed to ease the pain and it does dull its presence, but my grief is not so much painful as it is sorrow. I am confused about my sorrow and I feel guilty because I find that my sorrow is for more about me than my wife. At first I felt genuinely sorry for my wife. She lost a life too soon. Her death was sudden but it had to be frightening. I still feel that sorrow but I also miss my wife and I am sorry that she has gone and left me behind. Is that selfish or is that what grief is all about? If am just sorry because of my lonely situation then I ought to be able to do something about that to the extent that my grief will go away; shouldn't it?

I don't think it works that way. I would like to get away from some of the things that remind me of my wife's death. I can't drive by the hospital without the thought of that morning in the emergency room. I can't get rid of the recurring picture in my mind of my wife lying dead in that emergency room. Thank God I do not have a mental picture of her in a casket. I wake some times at night and, once again, live through that frightening three hours of a 911 call, the EMS crew, following the ambulance, the emergency room and finally the waiting room. These are the terrible pictures I want to remove and, hopefully time will do that.

There are myriads of good memories I want to keep. I will not forget how she looked. Her picture is in every room of my house. She monitors me. She nags me. She checks on what I am wearing. She loves me. I talk to her. I wish her good night. At my age I will not seek another companion. I think I will keep the one that I have.

Within a week after the funeral, you will be left alone. Now is the time for reflection, for sorrow, for remembering. You don't have to put on a brave face, carry on a conversation or do anything for house guests that have demanded your attention. It was probably good that for those first few days you did not have time to think fully about what has happened, but that day of reckoning is now at hand. Get outside; take a long walk, pray. Somehow you must come to terms with your loss. Your spouse's death was not God's will. Hopefully, it was no one's fault. Whatever the cause it is irrevocable and you must come to terms with it. I wish I could tell you how that is accomplished. I believe that living every day without your lifelong companion forces you to accept what your mind does not want to believe.

The loss of a longtime companion can be devastating in so many ways. Your grief must be accommodated and, over time, will be tempered. It will never go away—not fully, and many little things will come up that will trigger a memory; a snapshot, a hint of perfume, a place revisited, an envelope addressed to her, a mutual friend not seen in a while, a house full of triggers, a joke. A life together is full of so many memories that while time might ease the pain and mellow the loss, it will not erase a life together nor should it.

You will grieve uniquely. We are all different and how we are put together psychologically will determine how we suffer through the loss of a wife. I am not an outwardly emotional man. I have often wished that I could express my feelings openly and with sincerity, but for the life of me I cannot do it. Although I am hardly a cold fish, I believe that I am pretty logical and deliberate. It is part of my personality and it often frustrated my wife who certainly wanted me to be more open in my expressions of love and affection.

I am amazed by the people who can feel deep and genuine emotion over tragedies that do not touch or have a direct bearing on their lives. I was angered by the 9-11 attack on our country and appalled at the loss of innocent lives but I could not identify with the outpouring of grief professed by the millions of people who had suffered no personal loss by this attack. Surely, I knew how it hurt to lose a loved one, but knowing is not feeling. I am mystified by my lack of deep emotion when earthquakes, fires, landslides, hurricanes, tsunamis, and assassinations strike the lives of people I do not know while others not directly affected, openly weep and grieve. Am I some kind of insensitive slob? I certainly hope not.

I love the people I know. I care for them. I'm happy for them and I'm sad when bad things happen to them and I am, on those occasions, openly demonstrative about it but my openness is still, I must admit, reserved. And that is also how I grieve. I can cry in private but not in public. I can get teary-eyed, and still do, when I think of some nostalgic memory. I find now that I am more sensitive to loving and caring friends and family than I ever was prior to my wife's death.

"Time will heal your wounds," they say. I have heard this from many friends and when someone who has suffered a similar loss tells you this, you can believe it. But how much time before the wound is healed? Is there a scar? Of course there is and you would not remove it if you were capable. The pain of loss will recede into the back of your life but the memories won't dull. If anything they will be strengthened. My worst time is at night. The older you get, the less sleep you seem to require and I often wake in the night and, invariably, my thoughts turn to the life I had. Try as I might to keep my memories on the good side, I cannot yet get away from those awful last hours of ambulances and hospitals. When I get on this track, sleep is impossible but I have rigged a way to take my mind off this subject. I purchased a small television set for my bedroom, equipped with a speaker plug. A fifteen-foot extension lead plugged into a pillow speaker provides the distraction I need to get back to sleep. I tune the set into the Science Channel and set the volume so I can barely hear the commentary. I use the Science Channel because most of the commentary is in a monotone and the commercials are rarely loud and noisy. The light from the set does not bother me but a towel placed over the screen can block the glare. It may take sometimes as long as thirty minutes to get back to sleep but more often it is less. At least I do go back to sleep and who knows, perhaps I will pick up some knowledge, subliminally.

There can also be comfort in grief because, to a great extent, it is founded on memories, good memories for the most part. I recall my father whose daughters, upon his retirement, commissioned him to write a family history with the hope that this project would keep his mind active and his body busy. The project became a monster with Dad digging through old records, visiting cemeteries, calling old family members, and putting it all down in a Victorian style of writing that drove my editing sisters to distraction as they tried to shorten sentences that seemed to go on endlessly.

The history, when completed, was more memory than fact and, like most memories, it left out all of the bad stuff. If you were to read my father's history of his family, you would have to believe that our family, from 1640 to the present day, never suffered a divorce, never had a black sheep and included no drug addicts, alcoholics, murderers, or thieves. If there were any of these colorful types, they never got mentioned. The account encompassed four hundred years but most of the story told of my father's last 60: a happy flow of growth and prosperity.

Our own memories tend to be the most vivid when they are fond ones. Who wants to remember the crises and confrontations of life? This is why most of the memories we cherish of our partner are the good ones and they comfort us over our loss.

I am reminded of the lesson taught in the book written by Mitch Albom, *The Five People You Will Meet in Heaven*. The fourth lesson dealt with the principal character, Eddie, reuniting with his wife who had been deceased for some years. He was still bitter over the loss of his wife, which he believed was too soon. Ultimately he came to understand that his physical loss heightened his memory. A life was lost but the memory and love was not lost and he would have that forever. In like manner, my memories sustain me. They make me sad sometimes and happy at other times. Song lyrics that I never before connected to memories now have new meaning for me. *"Somewhere Beyond the Sea," "Softly, I Would Leave You Softly,"* are just a couple of the songs that now bring a tear to my eye and lump in my throat if I try to sing along with them. Love songs now just do me in and I have removed them from my car's CD player for fear that I will be distracted while driving.

I have heard it so often, it has almost become my mantra, that time will make things better, but I am not sure I want things to get any better. I am not sad all of the time and my sad times are less and less, but I would not erase a fond memory if I could. There is great comfort for those who have a religious faith for it provides a hope for the future. It has to be harder for a non-believer who must accept that their loved one lives only through the memories of friends. I do not know for certain that there is life after death or if there is what kind of life that is. But for now, at least, my wife is real and she waits for me. You can believe what you want.

I still talk to my wife every day. I greet her picture in the mornings and wish her goodnight in the evenings. I ask her questions and, having lived with her for over forty years, I pretty much know her answers. It gives me comfort to know that she is still watching what I wear in public and taking care of my personal appearance. When I look at myself in the mirror, my wife reminds me that I am going out in public looking like that and it gives me pause. I have gained a little weight. I can sense that she will be on my case if I don't start on a sensible diet. She is not a Pooh-Bah, because more often than not she is not as easy going as that giant rabbit, but she has let me slide a little bit. I hope that she approves of the way I am taking care of the house and the flowerbeds. I know neither is up to her standards, but then again, I never did do everything just the way she wanted. There is a little rebellion in any marriage and some of that carries over into grief.

I hope I have not been too maudlin on the subject of grief. Time may be a healer and too much time spent grieving is not good. A widower has more time than ever, especially if he is retired, and we will deal with this subject separately.

For now, a warning: don't dwell on your loss. Grieve in short bursts and move on.

I'll include a word here about books on grief. Most seem to identify specific stages of grief and they attempt to explain and justify each stage. I suppose I have gone through the stages of shock, denial, anger and acceptance but my experiences have not been one of stages like the steps on a ladder. My grief is all mixed up. I'm still in shock and I still want to deny that this whole thing has happened to me but I don't believe I was ever angry. Sad—yes. Who is there to get mad at? My wife for leaving me? Surely it was not her choice to do so. I can't blame God.

The God I believe in does not discriminatorily pick out people for death or sickness or the lottery. If there is any anger in me over my situation it is for my failures during our time together that bother me. What anger I have is directed against me for not loving enough, for not showing more emotion, for not expressing my love more often, for my lack of empathy in times of stress and for all of the things I wish I had done when there was still an opportunity to do them.

As to the stage of acceptance, what choice do I have? "The moving finger writes and having writ moves on nor all your piety or wit can lure it back to cancel half a line nor all your tears wash out a word of it." That line from the *Rubaiyat of Omar Khayyam* has stuck with me since high school and, sadly, it is all too true.

I cannot tell you how to grieve; I can only tell you that it is a necessary part of the adjustment process you will undergo in your new life. Let your friends share with you at this time. Do not shut out anyone who wants to help. You need the nourishment of sympathy that your friends and family are willing to give. You will be on your own soon enough.

3

Help From Family and Friends

I have three children: one girl, two boys and five grandchildren: four girls and one boy. Two of my children are technically step children but that category has long ago passed away. Although they have a caring paternal parent who is still very much part of their lives, I have by no means been treated as anything other than a father who enjoys their love and concern. All three are compatible and I have never sensed any discord among them nor have my wife or I ever knowingly granted favored treatment to any of them. Each has had his/her own needs and cares over the years but we have been blessed by children who married good men and women who, in turn, raised children that have earned our pride and love.

This happy situation makes me a poor advisor to men with families who did not experience a Brady Bunch upbringing, but unless you abused them or treated them heartlessly, you have the love of your children, however expressed. My wife's death has brought us much closer together. It was the first crisis that we all suffered through as a family and my children were magnificent. As a team they relieved me of most of the obligations one faces when a spouse dies, and they stayed with me until they felt comfortable in leaving me alone. My grandchildren were no less caring or helpful. They loved their grandmother as much as she loved them and they have since warmed a great deal toward their stoic old grandfather.

I have tried to ease the concerns that the children have expressed. They want to know about your health: not the details, but enough to feel comfortable about your living hundreds of miles away. I have wanted to get up on the roof to trim some tree limbs and have been instructed in no uncertain terms that I am not to perform that particular chore. I could hire someone to have it done, but it is such a small job that I hesitate asking for someone to take the time to bid on it. In order to placate my son, I shall wait until he visits and we can both get on the roof and cut the limbs. Why is it that I'm not certain that my 43-year-old son can do the job without me?

We talk on the telephone each week. I try to call before they do but they are still out and about on weekends running the errands that working people require to put off until Saturday or Sunday. So very little happens to me from week to week that I am afraid my calls are not very newsy but I believe it is important for them to know that things are normal. Communicate as often as possible to kids and grandkids. A computer and a cell phone are the devices of the day for people of my age. I-Pods are not for me but I can type and that makes e-mail a simple and easy way to communicate, especially when you want to tell everyone the same thing. The cell phone is also a great thing to have and while I don't use it often (I currently have 6,124 carry forward minutes) it does give me comfort that I can call for help no matter where I am situated. I am certain I would use it more if some of my children lived in the same town but I am able to call 911, AAA, the police and fire from anyplace I happen to be. I do not take pictures with the cell phone but I am capable of downloading and sending pictures via e-mail. I also bought an inexpensive digital camera, which has really been an added and pleasant means of communication that puts older methods to shame.

The children visit when they can and while we have not had a family gathering since Christmas, I have made it a point to see each one at his/her home and they have come to see me. Holidays are a concern. Working families don't have much time off even for holidays in America. It's too bad. We risk life and limb on crowded highways and travel hundreds of miles for a one or two-day Thanksgiving and a three-day Christmas visit each year. Other holidays, unless they fall on Friday or Monday, are generally too short. Since I have resolved not to drive long distances any longer, I plan to limit my holiday visits and encourage my children to enjoy their holidays at home where it is relatively safe. I can travel anytime and I want to choose times that place less stress on everyone. I have even entertained the idea of spending Christmas in Las Vegas to try to get beyond the sadness that this holiday inevitably creates in families where a significant loss has recently been experienced.

Although Christmas and Thanksgiving are times I no longer look forward to, they are, in spite of some sadness, a time of family togetherness and love. I wait, therefore, before each holiday occurs to decide on how I wish to participate. This sounds somewhat cold and deliberate but I have explained already that it is my nature and I would be less than honest if I did not express my feelings with the hope that my dilemma will be understood however I decide.

I do my best to include my children in decisions which I feel will affect them. Although I sense that they would rather not be included in a lot of them, they tolerate their roles as more active partners in my life and how I live it than they were in the past. They have yet, thank heavens, to assume a superior attitude toward my life, but as I get older I anticipate the time when I will have to yield to a few more suggestions as to what I should and should not do. I count the request that I not climb on the roof to trim the tree limbs as the first of these gestures. More suggestions, either direct or subtle, will most assuredly follow.

Grandchildren remain children regardless of age. They are the candy in your life. You can revel in their achievements and relive your youth once again through their adventures. You take pleasure in seeing your own children experience pay back for the misery and concern they brought upon you when they were your grandchildren's age. Much of the grandkid's love and attention to my wife has now come to me, not that I have earned it. Because they have lost the one who was by far the more attentive and active in their lives, they want to show their love for the one they lost by loving the one she loved. Does that make sense? They wouldn't tell you that but I know that I am more loved because their grandmother loved me than I am loved for what I am and that's just fine. The feeling is reciprocal in some ways, for I find that I must make sure that I now love them for both their grandmother and myself.

There is a fear that my new circumstances will bring about a change in relationship. The thought that I may start seeing other women and even begin dating has to be in the back of my children's minds. I know that after my sister died, my brother-in-law remarried. Actually over the course of some twenty years, he married twice more and these nieces and nephews have told horror stories about stepmothers who have separated their father from them and caused all kinds of problems with relationships and even inheritance questions. Could this happen to me? I think not. I admit I have a need for companionship beyond that of a golf foursome and a Sunday School class. While I did not seek out any females for almost a year after my wife's death, I have started going to some social events with a former friend of my wife whose husband died three years ago. Neither of us has any intention of allowing our friendship to develop beyond just what it is, a chance for interaction between friends of the opposite sex. That sounds stupid, I know, but I believe I can safely say that the possibility of anything beyond an occasional dinner, play or concert is not now in the picture or in either of our minds. Frankly, I am not interested in being any more involved with the opposite sex. I can take care of myself and I am not lonely most of the time, certainly to the extent that I would marry again to overcome it. The thought of starting a new life with someone else frightens and appalls me. I carry too much baggage from my past to put that away and start over.

Some men can handle this. There are plenty of widows to be found in my age group and some I am told are on the hunt. They are not looking for me, however, and that is just fine. I have enough pride to believe that I would be a pretty good catch, but my pride is not being wounded by the failure of widows flocking to my door. The fact remains that the need for personal relationships is found in each of us and I am not immune to it. My female friend has been a great sounding board for me as I am for her. We discuss our loss, we sympathize, and empathize. We talk and we know just enough about our respective pasts to make what we talk about easy to do without having to fill in a lot of background material. We are not "going steady" and are not inclined in this direction. We go out only when I can find an activity that appeals to both of us and this occurs only about twice a month.

I think that couples who are not married are still an exception in the social mix; especially among mature couples. You are seen with someone who was known differently when he or she was married just as you were also known differently. It takes a while for everyone to adjust. It's not the same. It is close, but just not the same.

Strangers will assume you are married. After all, it is obvious that you are old enough to be grandparents. I was asked to remove my wedding ring. My partner was sensitive to being perceived as being married to me. It was a sensible request. I had not thought of it, but, as a male, I fall into the category of failing to observe the many relationship nuances that are clearly obvious to members of the opposite sex. I was not hurt or insulted that she did not want to be thought of as my wife and I willingly removed it in deference to her request and with respect to my own wife.

We are still learning to be a couple both in public and in private. It was a while before I was willing to label our outings as "dates." Somehow the term does not have the right connotation, but, for lack of a better term, I suppose that we date. It's not like my courtship days but then again we are not courting. We just find it darn nice to be able to get together and talk about mundane things and enjoy whatever surrounds us.

I did not share this relationship with my children at first. It is not because I believed it was too soon for me to be doing this, but I was reluctant to offer even the slightest hint that I was betraying the love I still hold for my wife. They now know that I have a female companion and as far as I can tell, they are comfortable with the situation. Actually, they don't know much about this relationship and perhaps they are reluctant to inquire, but I hope that they neither view my actions as a betrayal of their mother or a change in my lifestyle that could materially affect them. Neither is the case, but life goes on and at this time I am undergoing some pretty drastic changes in that life which will require adjustments in attitudes on my part and on behalf of my children as well.

I am eighty years old. My outlook on remarriage, and dating is certainly different than that of a widower of fifty or sixty. No one expects you to remain single the rest of your life, and, unless you were a born a recluse to begin with, you will not wish to do so either. Thirty, forty or even fifty years ago you were dating or going steady. You met someone, fell in love and married until death do you part. Now you are at the beginning again. You are much more experienced. Surely you have learned how to please a woman. You have to learn to love someone new. I can't imagine how that feeling would be. I suppose it depends on so many things that it will be like the first time you fell in love but for a different, yet similar, set of reasons. Physical attraction, ideology, compatibility, religion, financial security all of these things were brought forth in your first courtship and they will occur again along with health concerns, family concerns (yours and hers) and estate concerns.

I have friends who have remarried after the death of their wife and, from what I can tell, they have achieved a happy and loving union. I remarried after a divorce as did my wife. Love for us was easier the second time around but we were young. I suppose it isn't a great deal different when you are old and in love. The peculiar thing about being old is that you don't think old for the most part. You are aware that you are eighty and your body won't do what you would like it to do but mentally you are still thirty-five; maybe forty. You don't picture yourself as what you really are and that cannot help but be a good thing.

Relationships with friends you have maintained for years as a couple will undergo a change. You are now the extra wheel. You will be left out of the loop for couples' activities unless it is known that you have the possibility of including a companion. Not a lot of activities for couples are instigated by men. Our wives got us together and, in our circle of friends, we did not get together all that often. We used to play quite a bit of bridge and in our early years it proved to be an easy and inexpensive way to entertain. A couple of tables of bridge, some dessert and coffee and the evenings were a success. I don't know what our children do to entertain other couples. They don't play bridge. We tried to teach them bridge but failed for their lack of interest. Now, when we get together as family we play board games or domino type games like *Spinner*, or *Balderdash*, or *Trivial Pursuit*. Do the children play these games with other couples? I think not.

Wives and widows still get together for lunch and for *Mahjong*, or bridge. But men, if they gather at all, do so for lunch or a game of golf or tennis. None of this goes on at night so your evenings become the challenge. I have set out to put together a social group of men, mostly widowers, but we might spike it up with a close friend who is still fortunate enough to be married. It would be ideal if we could meet twice a month for bridge or poker. With the addition of pie and coffee, how could we fail? Such a group also offers other obvious benefits aside from an evening's entertainment. While not everyone's situation is the same, the common ground would be our status as a widower, and it should be helpful to share our experiences.

I may have been too optimistic about this group but I believed it would afford those of us who have a need to repay invitations to parties and dinners a way to do this by underwriting a summer barbecue and a Christmas open house. We could pitch in and pay to have it catered and it wouldn't place a strain on anyone.

A list of widowers was completed and I got a cooked brisket from Sam's, a can of Ranch Style Beans, a container of potato salad, Texas toast, pickles, Videlia onions, beer, wine, and watermelon for an organizational meeting. The first meeting was a success in that everyone attended and had a really great time, but it failed to light a spark in anyone else for a subsequent meeting. For this group, at least, the common bond of being a widower was not strong enough to develop a support group of the type that I had envisioned. Happy to accept an invitation, there was not a real need among the group to feel that getting together on a regular basis would add to their current life-style.

I learned a valuable lesson. Even with the death of a spouse and an upheaval of their way of life, the average widower will remain within his own circle of friends so long as he will be accepted. Barring that, he seems content to exist as best he can within the environment which he is most comfortable. He will seek female companionship, and if not too set in his ways, even pursue a new-found love, but adding new acquaintances among his own sex will, at best, be a slow and reluctant process.

PART II
What Am I Going To Do?

4

When Everybody's Gone Home

There is work to be done in the aftermath of a death in your household. Acknowledging acts of kindness and messages of condolence was never my duty. Now it became one of the first wifely tasks I undertook. My wife was always insistent and persistent in acknowledging gifts and gestures. She had cards for every occasion and her grandchildren were welcome recipients of the cards and what else they might contain. For the most part, all I had to do was sign the card. Occasionally I would write a note when I had need of thanking a personal friend or person who had performed a kindness for me. In most of those cases I sent a card on which I had painted a watercolor. This gesture made the card and the thought that went with it more personal.

I resolved that in the case of responding to sympathy cards, memorials, food donations and other acts of kindness, I would write a personal note to each one. I purchased blank cards, which forced me to write because there was no printed message on the card. I wrote those notes for at least an hour each day until I got caught up. I found it comforting and not at all the chore I had imagined. It has opened up a form of communication I rarely ever used and I now find myself writing more notes and sending more cards than ever I did in the past.

Now there are a great deal of mundane but necessary changes you must make in your finances. If you have not taken care of your finances in the past, you must get assistance. A close friend whom you know that is knowledgeable in such matters, a banker, your lawyer-any of these can get you started, but remember you must learn to do your regular banking and bill paying yourself.

Is there a will? If not, what are the laws in the state concerning someone who dies without a will? It is obvious that you will need a lawyer. The bills keep coming and you cannot delay. You must have access to your bank account, the safety deposit box (if there is one) and the power to carry on your affairs. Your lawyer can get all of this accomplished. There will be questions regarding inheritance as well. Do you have stepchildren? Absent a will, are stepchildren treated differently by the laws in your state?

I am fortunate in that my lawyer lives next door. Of all of the people I meet, strangers and friends alike, my dog, Chester has not met anyone he does not immediately warm up to. Offer him a ride in your car and you could steal him in a minute. The one exception is my neighbor with whom he is very wary. It is odd because we can find no reason for it and, in fact, my lawyer neighbor looks after Chester if I leave town. I hope this is not a reflection of the legal profession because my neighbor has been an invaluable help in making sure that my affairs are in order. Changing your dual ownership's to single ones can get complicated and it is your responsibility to make certain that your affairs are in order so as not to be a burden to your children when you die.

At the same time that you are dealing with your lawyer you will need the assistance of an insurance agent to help you file any claims necessary for you to obtain settlements of these policies. Here, the agent who sold you the largest policy is probably your best assistant on all of your insurance claims. Hopefully, all of these policies are in one place. Each insurance company will have to be contacted, following which they will send a claim form which will call for a return of the policy, a copy of the death certificate, and a completed claim form. This all sounds easy but it will take you weeks to get these policies paid.

When they are, don't spend the money! Put it in the bank, a savings account, a credit union or with a stockbroker (if you already have one). The urge to pay off long term debts, especially the mortgage, is tempting but it is not advisable as your banker, if he is looking after your interests, will tell you. There is time enough to make a new financial plan.

Regular monthly expenses must be paid: the mortgage or rent, the utilities, the cable, the telephone, the service people, the maid. If you have been the regular bill payer and home accountant this will not be a problem but, if you have allowed your spouse to do all the bill paying, you are in for a session in basic accounting. Many people today are banking on-line. Some pay bills on line while others merely use the service for up to date review of their checking account. If you are computer literate I advise the use of this service if your bank offers it. Painful as it is, you will have to learn how to reconcile your bank statement unless you have more money than Midas and you keep too much of it in your checking account.

A budget is essential. You have to know what is coming in and what must go out. A review of last year's cancelled checks will be a good place to start if you don't have a clue about your finances. Once—a-year payments will sneak up on you if you do not anticipate them. Real estate taxes, income taxes, car insurance, and home owners' insurance are usually once a year or twice a year payments that must be considered. Monthly payments include life insurance premiums, credit card bills, mortgage or rent payments, utilities, cable, and telephone. Weekly expenditures include food, gasoline and housekeeping. All else is optional such as entertainment, and clothes. You must know what these items cost you and how you intend to provide the means to pay for them. If all of this confuses, you get help—quickly!

Do you have investments, retirement plans, Social Security? Ask your stock broker what, if anything, is needed to update your holdings. Does any retirement plan change with the death? How about Social Security, are you eligible? Was your spouse eligible? Take all advice with a grain of salt. Double-check it with a responsible person you trust.

Now that you are alone there are some protections you should consider. Have someone, preferably one of your children, made signatory on your checking account and safety deposit box. Power of attorney is not necessary in normal circumstances but your lawyer can tell you what is best in this case. You do need a living will, copies for which can be obtained from your hospital. You also need a medical power of attorney designating your children or a close friend to make medical decisions in your behalf if you are unable to do so. Copies of these documents need to be sent to all individuals who are named. A neighbor should have a key to your home and I would advise some means of getting help if you are suddenly incapacitated.

If a cell phone is not your style there are several monthly services available that will provide you with a means to call for help if you are unable to get to the telephone. I found a device in an advertisement that attaches to your telephone. Much like the monthly service call systems this one can be purchased outright with no monthly fee. It allows you to record a medical emergency message which will activate and automatically dial 911, providing pertinent information. In addition to 911 the system will then dial as many as five other people with the same message. This device can be activated remotely and as far as I understand it offers you the same protection as a monthly rental. While you may believe that your physical condition does not call for such a device, remember that you are now alone. You are not checked on everyday and if your children do not live in the same community, whatever action you take to protect yourself will be a comfort to them.

I recommend that you carry a cell phone with you at all times. If you don't have one, get one. An emergency call to 911 can be made as well as other calls for help in all sorts of situations. You can get help in setting up your cell phone and, besides that, any kid on the street can help you with using it or programming it if you get stumped.

Now that you are alone, security for you must become a bigger concern. The older you get the weaker you become and the more vulnerable. Be cautious in public. Don't expose yourself to darkened less populated areas. Dine out with friends—never alone. Investigate home alarm systems. If you don't want a pet, look for a recording of a big dog barking that you can set off behind a door. Install a motion-activated light in the back and front yard.

At some time you must reach a decision regarding your own insurance, life insurance that is. Obviously, you now have no need for life insurance except to provide a largess for your children or to pay off outstanding debts. I make the assumption here that your personal wealth is not such that you must protect your assets by life insurance. If this is the case, only tax accountants can help you since I have no experience with wealth of this significance.

I come from an era when ordinary life insurance was the thing to buy and so I bought it. As a result I have equity in these policies and was faced with whether or not to keep paying premiums on them. I had three choices: to continue paying premiums and thus maintain the insurance, to cash in the policies and reinvest the money, or to take paid up insurance and apply the premiums I had been paying toward debt, or investment. I chose the latter. My children are not wealthy but they are getting along. I should hope so. They are all over fifty years of age with grown children of their own. So maintaining insurance in order to provide a windfall at my death did not seem necessary. Cashing in the policies would require paying taxes on the money, which did not seem to be the smart thing to do because I do not need the money at this time. The paid up insurance idea fitted me best and I have informed my children of that move. I have maintained my supplemental hospital and health insurance along with some long term care insurance and I do have one small policy that I have had so long that the dividend pays the premium so I did not touch that.

Finally, having gone through the death of your spouse, you now should know what you should do to ease the problems you faced for those you leave behind. However much you have planned and discussed your wishes as regards what you want done after you are gone, it is best to write it down and place it with your will. You will save untold consternation among your children if they know specifically what you want done. Not only should this document accompany your will, it should also be available more readily by making copies for your children. Having experienced at least one death with which you have been personally involved, you should know what should be included:

1. To what extent do you wish to have your life extended in cases where you are incapable of making a decision?

    a. Maintain basic life support with pain relief

    b. Do whatever is necessary

2. Autopsy

    a. Only if required

    b. Provided the results could benefit others with similar deaths

3. Disposal

    a. Designated funeral home

        (1) Prepaid

        (2) Preference _____

        (3) No Preference

4. Carry a Whom to Contact in case of Emergency card on your person at all times.

5. Maintain a file covering all the things that need to be done in case of our death.

    a. Include numbers 1 through 4 above

    b. List of all insurance policies

    c. Investments/brokers

    d. Location of mortgage papers and all real estate records.

    e. Names and phone numbers of insurance agents, bankers, lawyers, ministers, housekeepers and service representatives

    f. List of all liabilities, including credit cards, mortgages, car loans and loans and miscellaneous obligations.

    g. List of all assets not included in any of the above.

    h. Make certain someone is signatory on your checking account and that they have access to any safety deposit box that you may maintain.

i. Include a copy of your up-to-date will

j. Funeral wishes

   (1) Full service

   (2) Memorial service/Military honors (if applicable)

   (3) Graveside service only

   (4) Viewing or closed casket

   (5) Cremation

   (6) Minister or spokespersons

   (7) Music

   (8) Scripture

   (9) Obituary (Write it yourself or have children do it)

   (10) Charities or other memorial preferences

J. Disposition of special personal belongings.

Wedding rings and such that cannot be equally divided nor sold must be allocated. Likewise, you may have assets o f value which are not readily recognizable as having any material worth. I have a watercolor print among a collection of watercolors that might appear to be just another print with little or no value. In this particular case, however, we happened on to its value almost by accident and found a treasure that I am certain the children would have missed. Years ago we had purchased this print of a group of pinto horses cleverly camouflaged against some snow-covered boulders. We paid $65 for it at the time and I framed it myself. Several years after that, my wife needed a present for a friend she knew who loved pinto horses so she called the gallery to see if she could buy another print. When told that it would cost $10,000 she told the dealer that she did not want the original but just the print. It turned out that this was the current price of the print. My last check on Ebay showed this limited addition print as being offered for $15,000 and change. I have taken care to inform the children of the value of that print and advised them to check on other prints we own, for they are probably more valuable than most of the trinkets and mementos we have treasured in the etagere.

Each person's assets, liabilities and wishes are different but the above list should trigger what additional information should be included in this "After-My-

Death" file. Review this file at least once each year. Your circumstances will change and this file should reflect the changes you may undergo. No matter how distasteful your children may find this whole idea, they will be grateful for this direction when that inevitable time comes to settle your affairs. If you are one of your children have a digital camera, and who doesn't these days, take photos of all of your material possessions that exceed your basic homeowner's insurance policy. Make a CD of these photos and place it in your deposit box along with your other valuable items and papers.

5

Stuff—Keep It or Lose It

If you own a home or a mortgage on one it is going to be hard to continue to live in it all by yourself and yet it is not something you should give up immediately, even if that is your intent. There is much to do. You have, over your lifetime, accumulated a lot of "stuff." It falls to you to do something about it.

Do you have any idea of what you store away in forty or more years? Neither my wife nor I thought of ourselves as savers. It is true that we did not undergo an annual garage sale clearance of unneeded clothes, furniture and bric-a-brac. We had one garage sale, which cured us of any desire to improve on this first disappointment. We had spent almost a week assembling our goodies and some were very good. I remember our big seller was a canopy bed that our daughter had outgrown. We had some pretty good furniture, having decorated with new stuff earlier. We put price tags on everything and arranged our items so that we could spread out onto the driveway with our display. We even ran an ad featuring our canopy bed.

We were ready for action on Friday night and truly anticipated a day of fun, profit, and lively customer relations. What happened was quite different and it cured me from garage sales for life. At six o'clock on Saturday morning the doorbell rang and a man stood on my porch wanting to know if I had a canopy bed for sale. I wasn't expecting this early invasion and I was definitely not prepared for what happened.

Putting on a bathrobe I opened the garage and before I was truly awake, I had allowed this man to pick my garage sale clean of all of the good stuff. What happened didn't really register until I got my wits about me and realized that I had been shopped by a re-seller. I was caught early and plucked clean by someone who did not want any of the items he purchased. He wanted them solely for resale and I had wanted to sell my goods to someone who really needed them and would use them. I felt bad about that transaction the whole day and swore that if

I ever needed to get rid of my possessions in the future I would give them away to some charity or agency that would place them in the hands of those in need.

I made two mistakes in conducting that sale. Advertising in the newspaper without setting the hours of sale left me open to early birds and not being able to recognize a cherry picker took the fun out of my day. I don't suppose resellers are doing anything wrong but the thought that this guy was going to take my stuff and make a profit from it just went against the grain.

Over the years when I have had the need to dispose of no longer needed or wanted clothes, shoes, TV sets, and gadgets of all kinds, I made trips to charitable agencies like Goodwill who will at least make good use of any profit they can derive from my discards. Now, however, I am facing a dilemma of somewhat larger proportions. Always before what we gave away was fairly small in quantity but now I am faced with three or four closets full of clothes and enough shoes to shame Imelda Marcos, the recognized shoe owner of the known universe. My first thought was to load all of it in the car and take it to some agency and let them dispose of it. But what agency? I decided to check them out. Nearly all of the agencies involved in charity don't just give things away. They sell them in stores they maintain for this purpose. Goodwill, Hospice, and many others make some money from the merchandise they sell and if you visit them, as I did, you will find that they are absolutely stocked to the ceiling with clothes and household goods. Frankly, I wanted to find an organization that would do as I was doing, give the clothes to someone in need, not sell them.

I don't deny that charities need the money but I wanted to find an organization that gives away what I am giving them to give away and that narrowed my search down to The Salvation Army, The Women's Protective Services and a number of church organizations. I finally selected The Women's Protective Services, a place where many women arrive with only the clothes on their back. My own church, while it performs local charity work, is not equipped or inclined to distribute clothing to the needy.

Obviously my choice of charity and my choice of giving, is not the only way to do this distasteful job. There are many organizations willing to accept your gift but when you do decide what to give, make certain that the items are clean and in good repair. Throw out the worn and overused items, all except the jeans. A walk through the mall of any city will convince you that the older, the more faded, the more torn a pair of jeans is the more in demand they seem to be.

If you find that you could use the money or if you happen to like the prospect of a garage sale, by all means organize a sale. You can then pocket the money or give it to a charity of your choice. I would caution you first to think about how you will feel about such a sale. A friend told me of his garage sale saying that it was terribly hard to sell his wife's possessions and that given a chance to do it again, he would find another means to give her things away.

Unless the presence of your wife's clothes brings about painful memories, I advise that you take your time and make a decision regarding these possessions deliberately. The empty closets may be a worse reminder than the clothes that hung in them. You have time to make this decision. It is not something that has to be done quickly.

It was nearing Christmas and an item in the church bulletin caught my attention. "We are in need of wrapping paper for use by the children's department," was the gist of the announcement. That hit me—I've got plenty of wrapping paper at home, I thought. I was up and down the attic steps every December, fetching paper my wife stored in the attic and her storage closet.

There are never enough closets in a home nor is there ever enough storage space, as any wife will tell you. My wife stored stuff in every closet in the house, but wrapping paper was confined largely to the attic and one of two closets we built in our hobby room off the den. We designed those closets so that we each had one for our own stuff. My wife's side was packed to the point that it overflowed onto my side. I was able to keep and sustain about 50% of my side, which is about par for the concept of husband and wife sharing. I knew there was wrapping paper in her space but I was unprepared for what else I found.

Here is a brief inventory: two cardboard filing boxes filled with used bows from former packages, at least half of a grocery sack of ribbon on spools and never used, 15 rolls of wrapping paper, a shoe box filled with Christmas tags, at least seven hand held tape dispensers, a bow tying machine with ribbon, Christmas paper plates and napkins, a four foot long Christmas table ornament, and two nativity layouts. Needless to say, when I arrived at their doorstep with this holiday trove the church was thrilled. This evidence points to our all-too-human characteristic of buying in anticipation of future need as well as buying new instead of checking to see if these things are already at home.

But that closet still had a Fibber McGee quality to it. The Fourth of July was another holiday we were over prepared for. The closet yielded American Flag motifs on place mats, napkins, plates, and cups. There were over 25 flags, which were used to line the flowerbeds and a floor mat to top off the collection.

I will not go into all the other items I found but did not dispose of, leaving those for the children to decide on at a later time. Some of the things kept there had everyday use: light bulbs, for instance, along with two clay crockpots, six boxes of jigsaw puzzles, extra tiles, grout, and grout cleaner for the kitchen and a box full of chew toys for the dog. At the very bottom of the pile was a real collector's item. A 22 x 16 inch poster, suitable for framing, of the George Bush inauguration, complete with a postage stamp properly cancelled to mark the day. What were we going to do with that?

All of this points to the fact that none of us wants to have a stranger go through our things. It is not so much that we have any secret love letters hidden away or anything like that. It's just that what we have accumulated and kept, for whatever reason, would be hard to explain or justify to anyone else. I am certain that my own closet full of necessities would be hard to explain or justify, as well, but even though I feel the necessity to clean out my half, I am reluctant to do it. If I keep putting it off, the kids will have to go through the whole mess instead of a filtered down collection of their mother's things.

The real purpose of this closet cleaning is to separate the wheat from the chaff. I wouldn't dare give away anything my wife had made or that the children might want, but I like to think I am doing a service, cutting in half what will have to be done when I am gone.

I come from a family of five children and we all faced the dilemma of what to do with our parents' possessions when our mother passed away. Here was a house filled with furniture and all of the other accumulations of a lifetime that had to be disposed of in some manner or divided up between us. How do you accomplish this in a civilized manner? We were all grown and married with children. We had no need for furniture, fixtures or even the house. Of course, there were some things of value and some things that had sentimental value to one or more of us.

We hit upon a solution that worked for everyone. We identified those items that were wanted by more than one of us and we put them up for a closed bid. The proceeds would go into the estate and be equally divided among the heirs. Mom's silver service, some cut glass, a few oriental rugs, and a few other things were placed on the auction block and each person submitted a written bid for the items they wanted. The items went to the highest bidder and, while I am sure there were some disappointments, everyone was generally pleased that the most valued items were disposed of equitably.

When no will specifies the distribution of valuables and there is no general consensus as to who should get a diamond ring, or locket, or picture, or keepsake, it is best to arrive at some suitable means of distribution in order to prevent the petty and sometimes hurtful arguments that can and do ensue. We have all heard the stories of some relative or in-law who, having arrived at the deceased's home first, helped themselves to things that were not theirs to claim. I know of one family that still holds their Aunt Martha responsible for making off with the family jewels to the point that they are determined, as a group, to deny her burial in the family plot, even though their grandfather had purchased ground enough for at least three generations.

I have heard of some people who have removed and disposed of all of their spouse's possessions, arguing that their presence is too painful a reminder of better times. My wife lives through my memories and I would not erase her presence in my life. Certainly her clothes should go, as should those things, which have the potential for use by charitable groups and agencies. But the personal belongings, jewelry, collections, travel treasures, the armoire's contents; all must remain for the children and grandchildren.

I have found that my children are reluctant to take anything of their mother's while I am still around. I'm sure it is a reluctance born of several beliefs. Taking something now makes death more final. It is the start of a separation that no one wants to face. There is a need to keep their idea of home intact. To remove something from it makes the home that they grew up in just a little less than they want to remember. I can understand that because I feel that way as well.

I have two automobiles that are fully paid for and in good running condition. One is a minivan and the other a four-door passenger car. I plan to keep both. I don't need two cars but they are both in good running condition and they serve two purposes in my life: one for golf and the other for more formal use. It sounds extravagant but I probably could not trade both of them for one newer more versatile model without a car payment to augment the trade and I simply don't want a car payment this late in life. I have never been a new-car buff. To me a car is just transportation and if it can accomplish that requirement then I am happy. I have resisted the more universal temptation of most men who are once again on the loose, to buy that convertible that was always a suppressed dream.

I feel compelled to begin the process of removing the extraneous things that were neither our children's nor mine. I'm not doing this in any hurried manner nor do I have a plan. I shall take it as it comes. My daughter-in-law made a wonderful suggestion and I am in the process of following up on it. She suggested that since my wife often wore colorful housedresses and colorful blouses, the material from them could be made into quilts or comforters for the grandchildren. I think it is a wonderful idea and I have contacted a person willing to make the quilts for me. So, before I find a home for my wife's clothes, the quilter and I will set aside enough material for her to do the job.

That now has me looking for other ways to utilize some of my wife's things in a manner that will be of help to others. For instance, while trying to find a quilter, I talked to a sales clerk in a quilting store. She mentioned work that she and others were doing for children who are victims of abuse and that led into my recalling that my wife had accumulated, during her sewing days, almost as much unused fabric in stock as she had Christmas wrapping paper.

I mentioned the fabric stash and was happy to discover that very good use can be made of all of this fabric by some quilters who provide a quilt to every child involved in the program. So now I have another project that can be undertaken. Not one of the children, nor grandchild has any inclination to take up sewing nor you can bet that the only use I will ever have for a needle is to dig out a splinter. My wife took up sewing with a vengeance when the grandchildren were little with the result that I now have two sewing machines, a serger, tables, patterns, scissors, needles, thread, and all of the extras that not one person in our family will ever use.

I have found a home for the cloth but now the need to find a good use for the other accoutrements of my former seamstress will lodge itself in the back of my mind. You just know that there is a good place for all this largess and it will come to me in time.

I have a friend who is a retired jeweler. He has promised to bring his loupe and come over and tell me what of my wife's jewelry is costume and what is real. I confess I cannot remember but once identified, the quandary arises as to the next step. Who gets what? When do they get it? Should I care?

I wish I had the answers. I wish my wife had given me instructions. I wish the kids would speak up. I hate to duck and run, to die and let whoever is left pick over the bones of our life. I like bola ties in my old age and my wife had a fairly large turquoise pin, which I believe can be made into a bola if it is turned sideways. That handles one thing. The real jewels, and there are not that many, become a true problem which I feel is my responsibility to solve while I still have my senses about me. Right now I sure feel dumb and numb!

So you see, I cannot cut and run from all of this. Not yet, anyway. Even if I wanted to move out of my house I could not do it without first cleaning out the clutter and calling in the children and having them take what they want. My daughter has agreed to spend a week with me for the purpose of going through the closets, cupboards, and chests sorting everything into the following groups: things to throw away, things that should be given away, things that other members of the family should look at before a final disposition decision is made, things that should be kept, things that, because of their obvious value, ought to be sold.

I suppose a sale of some kind is inevitable. Ebay is a possibility for some of the better things. Your children can help you here. If we decide upon a garage sale, it won't be clothes but it will be "stuff": crockpots, cooking utensils, dishes, glasses, vases, plastic flowers, games, card tables, extra linens, napkin rings, hammers, saws—the list goes on and on, I am not touching the visible things that make our house a home nor any of the things that will someday go to the children or grandchildren.

I know enough about garage sales to know that if you are going to have one you are going to need some help. Your children can provide that help by telling you what to keep and what to sell. In talking with one of the girls about what to dispose of that I will never use, she would make the comment, "one of the grandchildren will need that when they get married." It's nice to think that way but it is impractical. Not many newlyweds want someone's dishes or for that matter, even a practical item like a sweeper is for the children, they have "stuff" of their own and they are not looking for more of it. So help from family members must be tempered by reality and the decision of what to sell and what to keep must ultimately rest with you.

Once decided, additional help with organizing and putting on the sale will be necessary. There are professionals that do this for a fee but surely you have some friends who will give you a hand and, hopefully, their expertise. A friend who is not as close to these household items as family will be a great help in going through the house to pick out some things which ought to be included in the sale. Check out a few garage sales to get some ideas on merchandising and pricing. Pick a weekend that does not have conflicts with things that might take potential buyers away from your sale. Set the hours of the sale—NOT BEFORE 8 O'CLOCK and mean it—or the re-sale buyers will be upon you before the sleep gets out of your eyes. Be prepared to bargain especially late on the last day. Price everything, or in lieu of that, sort items by price and put them on separate tables. Have plenty of change, advertise, make a list to prepare by and lastly, do your very best to stay above what you are doing because a lot of your life and some items with great memories are being sold to perfect strangers who have no idea how they were acquired or how they were used.

But the question of moving sometime in the future lies before you and eventually, because of your age or your inability to manage a house, you must face the question of selling the home. If you do, where would you go?—To an efficiency apartment, a retirement home or village, or heaven forbid, to live with your children?

Financial ability as well as physical ability will dictate the answer. I am determined to remain in my house for as long as I can, but I have proved that I can take care of myself. Many men and women either do not feel comfortable doing this or for some reason feel the necessity to give up the responsibility of home ownership as soon as possible. My counsel, for whatever it is worth, is not to sell out too quickly. Where you are living now is probably the least expensive place you will find even if you have to pay now for services that were formerly done by your spouse.

I went to an open house of a new 600,000 square foot apartment complex containing one to four bedroom apartments. Shopping facilities, restaurants, covered parking, swimming pools, workout room, and a computer center were all part of the package but I was discouraged and vowed even more vehemently to myself that I will remain in my home as long as I possibly can. Moving from 3,000 square feet to 1,000 square feet is depressing. I may not utilize the space I now have but I enjoy rattling around in it too much to visualize myself along with what furniture I would be able to take into that tiny space. I have looked at garden homes with equal aplomb. Until I must have nursing care, my home shall remain my castle.

If you do plan to move, talk with your peers who have already relocated. State laws vary. Accommodations vary. Lifestyles vary. Visit locations. Talk to residents. What about moving to a city or town close to your children? Can you give up your church, your neighbors, and your friends? I know a couple that sold their home, moved away to a retirement village, stayed three months and moved back. They said they felt like they were fish out of water. Fortunately, they could afford the resulting cost. Before you make a change, ask yourself if you can make a drastic move away from the environment to which you have been accustomed? Make a change if you must but be very deliberate about it.

In summary, before you dispose of anything, involve your children in the decision. Don't rush into this process. Live with your possessions for a while so you can determine what not to part with. Depending on your financial needs, dispose of items in a manner that pleases you. If you plan to relocate, do your research even if it is only across town. Time is on your side.

6

Take A Skills Inventory

I am probably prejudiced but I believe that the person who is generally less equipped to being left alone is the male. A widower, especially if he is over sixty does not have the skills to live by himself. Not if he has enjoyed a loving and caring wife who cooked his meals, washed his clothes, made his bed, coordinated his colors, mailed his birthday cards, kept in touch with his family, reminded him of appointments, and loved him. Oh, he helped at home. He carried out the garbage, cooked a steak on the barbee, set the table, and even ironed a shirt now and then and, when asked, ran the vacuum cleaner. Regardless of your current skills as a housekeeper, you will need to make adjustments in order to fill in what you rarely if ever performed.

You will need to take stock of your household skills. I am pretty much an organizer so I make lists. The following checklist helped me take inventory of the practical skills I believed were going to be needed. It would help you to make such a list or fill out this one. Remember, I am not talking here about your golf swing or your ability to pat your head and rub your stomach at the same time—you need to know what you can do to make your everyday life go smoothly. Be honest.

PRACTICAL SKILLS INVENTORY

Cooking:_____

  __Can boil water and thaw a frozen dinner
  __Can grill steaks, fry an egg, make toast and coffee.
  __No gourmet but able to follow a recipe
  __Can prepare a balanced meal
  __Can do a candle light supper

Cleaning:

    __Can run the vacuum cleaner
    __Can load and run the dishwasher
    __Can load and run the washing machine
    __Can load and run the drier
    __Can clean toilet bowls, sinks, countertops, windows,
    __Can clean carpet stains
    __Can clean the dishes/pots and pans

Maintenance:

    __Able to change the sweeper bag
    __Able to unstop the toilet
    __Able to clean the aerator on the faucet
    __Able to reset the switch on the fuse box
    __Able to unstop and restart the food disposer
    __Able to defrost the refrigerator (if necessary)
    __Able to reset the clocks
    __Able to reset the thermostat
    __Able to light a furnace pilot light
    __Able to change filters

PRACTICAL APPLICATIONS INVENTORY

Service Providers: (Who to call and the telephone number)
Plumber
Electrician
Pest Control
Yard or Lawn work
Painter
Security System
Housekeeper
Things to do:

    Once a year
    Seasonally
    Monthly
    Weekly

The Date Book:

Essential Calendar Entries

    Birthdays (Children {include year of birth}, friends, relatives, pets)

    Anniversaries (Children, friends, relatives)

    Memory Days (Children, friends, relatives)

    I cannot emphasize enough that you maintain an address book and a calendar in which you record every event of significance in your and your children's lives. If you do not have such a calendar I suggest getting a three-year calendar and posting these dates into the future. You will be adding to this calendar as events occur that will require notation. Don't forget your wedding anniversary and even the date of your wife's death. Memory is a peculiar thing and as time goes by you might pass over a significant date that used to be unforgetable. I regret to say that I cannot tell you the year, much less the date, of my siblings' deaths. I intend to post those dates in my calendar for it will give me a nostalgic reminder of that loved one whose memory slowly passes. If dates of death are not reminders you wish to keep, then by all means, post the birthdays of those who are gone.

    I have already written about the address book that my wife kept. It is absolutely essential that you maintain this record for this is a secretarial duty that you must now assume. Before you erase your wife's address book on the computer, be sure to check it for people she may not have posted elsewhere.

    Having now completed your check lists and updated your address book and calendar you should have a better idea of your strengths and weaknesses and it is now time to tackle the job of living alone.

7

Free at Last?

When you are widowed it is easy to get caught up in self-pity, loneliness, grief, or all of the above. It is doubly difficult if you are retired when this situation befalls you. Having a job to go to at least provides the discipline to maintain a life-style that includes getting out of bed, putting on clothes, and going out in public. The retired widower has little or no demands on his performance and it is easy to turn into a slob. (People who are slobs already won't read or buy this book)

After all, who cares? Why make the bed? For that matter, why even change the sheets? Is there a reason to shave every day? Why cook?

It is darned easy to become a slob and it takes discipline to establish a life-style that continues what you have had all of your life. However you may have lost your spouse you will discover soon enough that without the need to be a companion, a lover, a helpmate, a supporter, what you accepted as the required way of doing things is no longer required. When that happens, it will be time to establish your single life-style.

Get a dog if you don't already have one. If you do not want a dog, at least get a pet. A cat will do—something small that will get in your lap, but more importantly, will make constant demands on you for food, water and exercise. A dog won't replace a wife, although there are some who would argue otherwise, but it will not only be company but it will require your attention and that is important when you are alone most of the time. An added benefit is that your pet will listen when you talk and, as far as you will be able to tell, agree with you in every instance.

All breeds have their supporters and far be it from me to seek to influence your selection of a dog, I prefer poodles. All pets assume the characteristics of their masters. If you are active they will be active, if you are gregarious they will be friendly, etc. Poodles have one advantage over most breeds. They don't shed. That is a blessing you will soon appreciate when it comes to maintenance of both the house and the animal. A dog door is essential although I know many people who do not have one and their pet seems to adapt to this confinement. My dog has the run of the house and the back yard and, accidents are virtually eliminated. If I take a weekend trip my neighbor comes over and feeds my dog this is all he really needs. This past Christmas our whole family joined me and they brought their dogs. There were 12 people and seven dogs and snow! Fortunately it was cold enough that the in-and-out traffic through that door, although considerable, failed to leave a trail of muddy tracks because the ground remained frozen. One of the dogs was not familiar with a dog door but he learned in about one minute. Installation of such a door in the mudroom (for you Yankees) would be an ideal location.

Establish routines as a way to keep yourself orderly. Find ways to participate in activities that require regular attendance. A later chapter will describe in more detail ways you can maintain your participation in the human race. But for now, shave every day, brush your teeth every day, put on clothes every day, straighten your bed at least if you don't want to put on a spread, and hang up your clothes. Do I sound like your wife? It is important that you continue to take care of yourself because you are the only one left to do it and it is so easy to let the little things slip. Keep a photo of your wife in the bathroom. Her presence will help you maintain your pride as well as your physical appearance.

8

Polishing the Silver

Whether you live in a house (as I do), or in an apartment, someone will have to maintain it and, to a great extent that assignment now belongs to you. The responsibility for maintaining your clothes, cleaning, dusting, yard work and cooking is going to help fill up your day.

We have discussed cleaning out the closets and getting rid of things that no longer apply to your life. But the house is more than closets and, while there is not that much that I feel compelled to dispose of, there is quite a lot that needs care and it needs it frequently. Most men, me included, do not do housecleaning and what little we do, we do without enthusiasm and it shows.

I advise the obvious—hire a maid for once a week, twice a month, or at the very least, once a month. In my own case, we already had a maid and she does a good job, I think. How would I really know? I can see evidence that she cleans the bathrooms, my bedroom, the sheets, the kitchen floor and she vacuums the house. I know that her work pleased my wife to the extent that any housekeeper could please her. From complaints I heard voiced to me and not to the housekeeper, she did not use a hospital fold on the bed sheets. I am continuing to struggle with that. For the life of me I cannot tell what difference folding the sheets at the bottom of the bed had to do with a good night's sleep.

Cleaning a 3,000 square foot house in four hours every other week is probably just keeping the mold and dust mites at bay. Over time, I'm sure problems will compound but I am counting on someone to notice and let me know what else needs to be done. I don't walk around with a white glove inspecting the house but I suppose I should look for some little things to do just to keep the housekeeper aware of my continued diligence.

I wonder if she has blinded my inspections with something akin to copper wire. You see, it takes a thief or, in this case a slacker to catch a slacker. Friday was clean up day in the Navy, and I was a radioman on a battleship in World War II. My cleaning station was a small room that contained a row of transmitters each the size of a refrigerator. The room was small, about six feet deep by twelve feet wide. Traffic in this room was nil. When I closed the hatch each Friday I knew that it would be exactly one week before anyone would enter that room and most likely that person would be me.

It was the greatest cleaning assignment on board the ship and only through some snafu did I get the job and I sure wasn't bragging about it to anyone. Every Friday when they blew Turn To on the Bosun's pipe and announced, "Now hear this, all hands turn to, we want a clean sweepdown fore and aft," that meant that all hands were to man their cleaning stations and start to work. I dutifully entered my transmitter room, checked for any dirt on the deck and sat down and spent my time reading *Forever Amber*. It did dawn on me that there was a remote possibility of an inspection, which might point up some nitpicking thing that needed to be done. To offset any inspector from reaching up to the top of the transmitter with his hand as a check for cleanliness, I got some bare copper wire. I arranged it carefully on the top of the transmitters so it looked every bit a part of the equipment and a dangerous and potential shocking part, at that. The wire worked as far as I know because no one ever put a hand up on top for fear of electrocution or, at the very least, a severe shock.

Knowing about copper wire scams, I now wonder if the maid has done it to me in some other way. It doesn't matter; the house will not be as clean if she quits. Could it be cleaner? I suppose so but for now, it passes my inspection, which avoids the copper wires if there are any.

Cleaning a house every other week will not get the everyday job done and you will find a need to keep up or face an ever increasing accumulation of debris and muck that will soon turn your nest into a disaster that your housekeeper will not accept money to repair. Habits of a lifetime should not be abandoned now.

"Pick up your clothes." Do you remember your mom telling you that over and over again and I'll be darned if that sweet thing you married didn't have the same habit as your mother. Of course, when the kids came along, you could get even. They had to pick up their clothes as well which allowed you the privilege of enforcing this rule on the lesser members of the pecking order. The absence of pressure to be tidy, neat, clean, to shave every day can lure even the best of former husbands into the role of dirty old men.

Maintaining the set of standards you had as a couple is truly necessary to peace of mind, especially early on in your new single status. "Time is a great healer"; I am told repeatedly by people with good intentions and by some that have the experience to back up this axiom. But time takes time and that first year of living alone should not include any more drastic change than is necessary. Do what you have always done plus what you must now take over and keep as much order in your life as possible. It will make the grieving more personal and by that I mean that you will focus on your loss of a companion, a confidant, a lover, a friend rather than a housewife, a maid, and a laundress.

That brings up another new responsibility that I doubt very seriously you shared during your marriage—the responsibility for doing the laundry. I got a lesson in laundry because my wife was handicapped with foot surgery. I am certain there is more to it than what I was taught but she taught me enough that I now launder my clothes without any more trouble than the time it takes to accomplish the task.

Here are the basics. Separate whites from colored clothing. Send dress shirts, suits, and dress pants to the cleaners. Specify the amount of starch in the shirts from zero to heavy. My wife had me separate my underwear from the rest of the whites so they would be washed with bleach. Wash colored clothes including towels, slacks, sweats, and sport shirts in cold water. Detergents, I am told, will do an adequate job of cleaning in cold water and you can now purchase detergents specifically designed to wash clothes in cold water. Watch it with the detergent. Look at the size of the load. Too much detergent and the rinse cycle will never be able to remove all of the soap from the clothes. The label on the back of the container won't help you much but I suggest that you add soap on the side of caution. Use a lid half full for small loads to a full lid for a full washer. This applies to whites as well.

When washing whites, be sure to add the sheets. Since most sheets are now made with a fitted bottom sheet, changing your sheets and pillowcases by yourself shouldn't be too much of a chore. There is a linen closet somewhere in the house and at least a second set of sheets available so plan on rotating them. Underwear should be washed in hot or warm water and my wife had me add some bleach to the water even though most detergents have some kind of bleach in them. The amount of bleach I was inclined to add would take the color out of a black pirate flag. Use a small amount, about a quarter cup, with the detergent and this should do the job. You don't want your underwear to smell like bleach so give the rinse cycle a chance to do what it is designed to do. There are also stain removers, which can be safely applied to any stain on your clothes just prior to the wash. It is helpful to allow the enzymes in these removers to activate before you start adding water to the wash.

Look at your washing machine. There is a place to add liquid softener in the washer or you can add a sheet of it in the dryer. I prefer the latter but I don't get carried away. Women like things softer than men do and I used to think our bath towels were soft but less absorbent. I really don't want soft in a bath towel; I want absorbent. Softeners are up to you and if you have had no experience or training in washing clothes, stay on the low side.

Drying the clothes should also lean to the less heat and longer cycle than is high heat and short cycle. Use nothing higher than warm and just choose the time cycle settings instead of trying to determine whether you are drying permanent press or whatever. Start with fifteen or twenty minutes. You can always add time. You can dry everything, colored and white together but this is not very efficient. Dry the colored clothes while washing the whites, then fold the colored clothes while the whites are drying. About two months after I assumed the clothes washing duties my drier started screaming. At least it developed a high whine that sounded like an un-oiled bearing or a loose drive belt. Nothing else seemed wrong and, in spite of the noise, the drier worked fine. I tried to open the back of the drier but there are at least three layers of panels you must go through to get to the guts of the machine. I gave up after peeling off two layers and screwed everything back together, vowing to run the drier until it burned up or died. It was getting old anyway and I could afford a new one before I wanted to pay some repairman a fortune for coming out and flipping some switch with which I was unfamiliar and walking away with my pride and my first hour fee.

The next time my son paid a visit, he washed some of his clothes and heard the drier. "Dad," he said, "the lint filter is full and is causing your drier to make a noise." Who knew? So I saved a repair call. Now I empty the lint filter on a regular basis and hear no more screaming drier. Your drier has a lint filter. Look for it. The filter is not in the same place in all dryers. If you happen to make paper, which I did back when I was painting, you can throw the lint into the pulp mix. Otherwise, toss it. Dryers are notorious for eating socks. It's a great wash day if the socks come out even and pairing up socks are one of the more entertaining functions of doing laundry. I usually find my lost socks in the pocket of some pants or tucked in a pillow slip but some socks have totally disappeared and any woman will swear to the mystery of the sock-eating drier.

Folding clothes calls for very little if any skill. The only real challenge comes in folding something bigger than your arms can reach. I lay sheets out on the floor until I can get them folded small enough to pick up. This violates the housewives' code, I know, but some modifications have to be made in order to accommodate my male dexterity, and the fact that it is hard to get your neighbor to come over and help you fold clothes. Do not attempt, I say, do not attempt to fold a sheet with fitted corners. Only the little oriental girl in the Far East factory knows how to do this and she is highly paid because without her they would never get this sheet in an 18 x 18-inch package. Just fold it enough to fit in the linen closet (better yet, let the maid do it). The beauty is that when stretched over the mattress, most of the wrinkles will disappear.

Here are the instructions I copied for folding a fitted sheet provided you have two people:

Step 1. Turn sheet upside down, and from underneath tuck fingers up in tips of hemmed corners.

Step 2. Walk backward until sheet is fully extended.

Step 3. Bring your hands together; and neatly tuck one corner into the other. Turn the sheet parallel to floor; and fold edges down slightly to create a straight line.

Step 4. Fold lengthwise, bringing hands together again.

Step 5. With sheet parallel to the floor, walk toward your partner for a fold, then fold in half twice more.

As you can see, even with two people the job is virtually impossible. You and the maid can give this try if you are a true neat freak but I do not guarantee the result. In addition to folding sheets, you will have to fold some of your clothes. I cannot help you fold clothes. I do know that most of your pants and shirts will do better if you put them on a hanger when they are first removed from the dryer. Socks, towels, underwear, t-shirts and the like need to be folded to save space. I like to roll up my undershirts and t-shirts. They store so much easier although now you probably have more drawer space than you will ever need and you can spread out without being concerned with space requirements.

Most of my shirts are of the sports variety. Since I no longer have need for a dress shirt every day, I don't have to iron a great deal. Besides that, I would send my dress shirts to the laundry, anyway but I can iron if I have to and before I iron, I have to. Ironing is a challenge but I have found that the challenge lies in how you place the item on the ironing board. A shirt requires multiple positioning and very little actual ironing. The old crease in your slacks will give you some guideline. My suggestion is to hang up your pants and put on some casual slacks when you are home alone. You can get quite a bit of wear out of one dry cleaning if you are careful with your clothes. If, however, you are a clotheshorse, then I cannot help you. Be prepared to spend whatever it takes. This was probably an expense you were already incurring.

There are other maintenance household duties that will come to you as you walk through the house. Do you have any houseplants? If so, they will need water regularly. My house is not designed for live houseplants. There are no sunny spots. Windows that face the South are either in the bedrooms or shaded by a porch. My wife, always the optimist, would bring plants home to die. Some died slower than others but all died. We have some silk flowers and plants in the house and they are doing okay so far. I knew the problems of keeping live plants in this house, so when I received a number of pot plants during and after the funeral, I kept them for about a week and then found a home for each with friends I knew that would give them the care they deserved.

Water softeners need tending. Toilets need flushing. If you have more than one bathroom and they are not all in use from time to time it is essential that you flush the toilet so that the seals will remain resilient.

Anything that has a filter will need attention from time to time. Your smoke alarms should be tested and the batteries changed out twice a year. Someone suggested doing this when daylight-saving time changes but if they keep extending the times it is in force you might find another plan that will work as well. Entering it into a calendar on your computer is the best way. A lot of these things like yard work and general maintenance you are probably already doing and you will have to keep it up. Try to remember what things your wife did that did not concern you and add them to your list of regular chores.

Sanitation is essential. Keep your bathroom and kitchen clean on an as used basis. Don't allow spills, drips, and drops to accumulate. Wipe down everything periodically with a spray cleaner that contains some bleach or disinfectant. Check the refrigerator and the freezer for leftovers that have been left over too long. The produce drawer should be removed and cleaned periodically. Change out your drinking glass frequently and pre wash your dishes before placing in the dishwasher. I know the dishwasher is supposed to remove everything but if you don't run it everyday, food particles will dry and stick to the surface of your dishes. The dishwasher won't clean them after that.

All of this new responsibility can create a real desire to move away from it. But think for a minute. Even if you move into a limited care facility, most of these chores will still go with you. You might not have to cook every meal but I'll bet there will be a toaster oven or a microwave, a refrigerator, and a sink. You will still be paying for maid service and it will probably be more expensive than a once a month visit. So long as I have my health I will opt for staying in my home and taking care of myself and my surroundings. After all, if you are not still working, you are going to be looking for things to occupy your time.

PART III
The Time Consuming Business of Eating

9

You Can't Eat at McDonald's Everyday

The time will come, and it will be sooner than you think, that the casseroles given to you by sympathizers, peanut butter sandwiches and Big Macs will grow old and you will need to start cooking for yourself. It is essential to maintain order in your life and that includes cooking or meal preparation. You don't have to cook a meal every day but you do have to eat every day and that calls for planning. The fridge, the freezer and the pantry should provide you with the where-with-all to accomplish this feat. Regardless of your skill level, some analysis needs to be made of your existing situation before you can feel comfortable in the kitchen. Follow these suggestions:

Step One: Clean out the pantry. There will be stuff in there you will never eat. Reduce your pantry to the basic things you like and feel like you will be able to use. Box up the rest and give it to the Food Bank or similar charitable organization.

I often put up the groceries for my wife after we had gone to the grocery store. It was always a challenge to find a place to store what we had just bought. You had to ask yourself, "Why did we go to the store in the first place?" Surely we could have made several meals from the cans, boxes, and packages already stuffed in the pantry.

Having now examined my pantry with a more critical eye, I now believe I know why our pantry was so full. We all buy on impulse in the anticipation of need and for whatever reason those clever marketing execs have brainwashed us into. When I started to pare down my pantry to the essentials, I found 7 cans of condensed milk, 6 packages of chili seasoning (my wife always made chili from scratch, never from a package) 3 bags of pickling salt (we never pickled anything) and an old Seal-a-meal machine complete with the bags. I now regret having given this item away after watching the Antiques Road Show. I just know that thing has quadrupled in value. Incidentally, I just bought a new food-sealing machine and use it quite frequently.

Step Two: The same goes for preparation utensils. Get rid of the garlic press, the drawer full of gadgets that you don't understand and will never use. When you cook for one you will need only the basics:

Paring knife
Vegetable knife
Bread knife
Serrated knife, medium
Small, medium and large carving knives
Two prong fork

Two spatulas, wide and narrow

Rubber spatulas, three sizes
Mixing spoons, plastic, metal and wood
Whisks, small and large
Can Opener and a Church Key
Butter knife or spreader
Corn cob holders

Knife sharpener

Jar vice
Cheese grater
Measuring cups: one-cup size and two-cup size
Tongs
Cheese cutter
Cutting boards, green for vegetables, blue for beef and pork, yellow for chicken, white for miscellaneous use.
Meat thermometer
(I'm certain that I have forgotten something)

* These boards (actually you will probably have nylon or some plastic type material), must be sterilized frequently along with the sponge you may use to clean your kitchen counters. While the dishwasher will do a pretty good job, I suggest you microwave each one for one minute on high to complete the job.

If you have been married any length of time you will be surprised at what you will have left over. Put all of these items in a box. Who knows, you may need one or two as your cooking skills develop. For the time being, it is important to eliminate as much clutter as possible.

Step Three: Cooking utensils need to be eliminated as well. Your skill level determines what you need. For the beginner I suggest the following:

> One set of sauce pans with lids
> Two non stick frying pans, small and large
> One set of mixing bowls (microwaveable)
> One set of Pyrex or oven proof lidded casserole dishes
> One two burner iron grill or one of the new electric grills
> One set of mixing bowls (microwaveable)
> One set of Pyrex or oven proof lidded casserole dishes
> One two burner iron grill or one of the new electric grills
> One large pot (for chili, soup and stew)

Put the rest in a box in the garage. If you are a beginning cook, it will be a long time before you have to open that box to get a turkey roaster.

Step Four: Appliances will abound in any kitchen that has been around any length of time. Mixers, graters, cutters, grinders, toasters, fryers, convection ovens, sandwich presses, waffle irons, apple peelers, microwaves, slow cookers, coffee makers, blenders, and a myriad of labor saving and time saving devices all compete for storage space and infrequent use. You will use a few of these repeatedly and the rest, hardly at all.

If you have them, keep these handy:

> The microwave
> The coffee maker (You might want to look into the new one cup units)
> The toaster
> The toaster oven
> Crockpot or slow cooker or both
> An electric or stove top-grill

Put the rest of what you have out of the way but don't get rid of them. Who knows? You might want to pull out the manual for the Cuisinart and see if you can chop up an onion. You will find that the preparation and clean up time aren't worth what little time you will spend on a chopping board.

Step Five: Eating and serving utensils also need paring. If you have crystal, china, and "the good silver," don't use it! Maybe the kids will take it. Put it away. You will need: a set of six plastic or inexpensive china plates, soup bowls, salad bowls, cups, saucers, six to ten glasses of various sizes from juice to iced tea, wine glasses & brandy snifters if you are so inclined. A set of six or eight stainless steel place settings, plus a few serving spoons, one large wooden or plastic bowl for tossing salads and three or four serving plates.

Step Six: Storage containers will be helpful. Get a variety and make sure they will work in the microwave—some small enough to hold a half a can of peas, beans, corn, and some that will hold one to two servings and one or two that are larger. Make certain that all have lids. You will also need a variety of plastic bags preferably suitable for the freezer. Add packages of aluminum foil, waxed paper, paper towels and plastic wrap. Some foods, principally onions and potatoes, should not be refrigerated and should be stored separately in a wire basket in the pantry. You will also need a bowl for holding fresh fruit.

10

The Tools of the Cooking Trade

(A primer for the neophyte)

If you are working from an established kitchen, don't throw anything away just yet. Set all of the rest of the stuff out of the way, preferably in another room, and learn to work with what has been suggested. The cooking basics include heating, toasting, broiling, frying, and baking. Let's take these one at a time.

Experiment with what devices you have that can be used to heat food. I have discovered the following:

<u>Microwave</u> … It will warm almost anything quickly. Be sure that no metal is placed in the unit and always put a cover over the object to be heated. Water will heat but this is done better on the stove. I have been told that a microwave heats from inside out so stopping the microwave while it is heating and stirring the contents will give you a more uniform heat. It is best used to defrost frozen dinners and stuff from your freezer. All frozen dinners and other items provide heating instructions for their product. Follow the instructions and in the case of items from your own freezer, I advise using less than 100% when you thaw something. That way, you will avoid cooking something again that you only wanted to warm. I think a microwave makes meat taste different if it is overheated or over thawed. To thaw meat it is best to put it in the refrigerator the night before you want to use it. That way, it will thaw gradually but still remain cold.

A microwave will cook some things but I don't recommend it for anything but popcorn, oatmeal, and mashed potatoes made from potato flakes. I do find that it will do a good job of steaming either fresh or frozen vegetables and is very good for heating canned vegetables. It will cook a potato but it makes it gummy. Plan a little ahead and bake that potato in the regular oven. You will get a better product. If your microwave does not have a turntable it is a good idea to stop the heating process about halfway through the timing and turn the item around in order to get more even heating. "Microwave Cooking for One" can be pulled up on the Internet and, if you are interested, you can order the book.

Toasting:

<u>Toaster</u> ... What can I say. Sliced bread, English muffins, and bagels (provided the slots are big enough) are all the toaster is good for. Do not spread or sprinkle anything on the items to be toasted. For that, you need a toaster or convection oven.

<u>Toaster Oven/Convection Oven</u> ... This is a great appliance for the person who cooks for just one or two people. It will bake, toast, or broil and if it has the convection feature (which is a fan that stirs the hot air around and therefore cooks faster) you can speed up the process over your regular oven. Without the turbo or convection feature, the oven cooks in about the same time as your regular oven but when cooking for just one or two people it is not nearly as messy. The toaster feature allows you to melt butter on your bread or make garlic toast with garlic sprinkle. By the way, you can now buy garlic bread in the frozen food section of your grocery store. This allows you to heat one or two slices without having to purchase a whole loaf of French bread.

<u>Broiling or Grilling</u>: This is just like using the outdoor grill except that instead of cooking from the bottom you will be cooking from the top. Broiling is messy and I think meat tastes better grilled. You won't be needing to broil at all until your cooking skills are more advanced. Grilling is different. Almost everyone can grill a hamburger or a steak, but going outdoors and firing up the grill is a hassle. So I suggest you buy a cast iron unit with a grill side and a flat side for frying that fits over two of the burners on your range. It is a mess to clean but if you follow the instructions for curing the cast iron, you should be able to clean it with a mild soap and plastic scrubber. Don't put it in the dishwasher. The harsh soap will remove the cure you have been cultivating.

Electric grills do the job just as well as the cast iron grills and are probably easier to clean. Use what you have; don't buy one just yet. A George Foreman Grill or comparative brand electric grill would be a great addition to your cooking equipment if you do not already have one. Get one with removable grill plates for easy clean up. This grill will cook a steak, hamburger, fish, chicken breast, or pork chop with less effort and mess than grilling on the stovetop. Timing will require some trial and error but err on the less time side than over cooking. You can always put it back on the grill in one-minute intervals and then make note for the next time around.

<u>Frying</u>: The big danger here is getting the pan too hot to begin with. Unless you want to sear whatever you are frying, a medium burner setting is best. Eggs fry better in medium heat and it will give you time to flip the egg if that is your choosing. Putting a lid on the pan will speed up the process and after I sear the

meat (like pork chops) I turn down the heat and put a lid on the pan. The chops are well cooked and the grease spatter is lessened. I believe chicken tastes best when fried but it is probably the least healthful for you. There are a lot of batter recipes for chicken and fish. Ask a friend for theirs or buy one of several available at your grocery store.

Baking: Most things you will bake (and it won't be much) will probably come with baking instructions. Follow them. You can use your oven to warm things in lieu of a microwave or toaster oven. Hopefully you will still have the booklet that came with the oven; if not, trial and error or a knowledgeable friend can help you set the temperature, and even the timer if you want to get sophisticated. I like the oven for some cooking that I find cumbersome in a toaster oven.

The dairy section of your grocery store is abundantly supplied with biscuits; cinnamon rolls, cookies, and yeast rolls all packaged and ready to bake. Baking corn bread from package mixes is easy. For this job I recommend using a cast iron skillet and if you put the skillet in the oven as it heats to the temperature setting, your corn bread will bake with a nice crust on the bottom.

Slow Cooker: This is another great appliance. You can dump in the meat and vegetables, add seasoning, set for four to six hours on fast or eight to ten hours for slow cooking and forget it. It is pretty hard to fail with this one and you can cook beef, pork, chicken, lamb, stews, chili, soups, and chowders and it will do it without any attention on your part once you have loaded it up. The Internet can give you a lot of ideas for using this device and the pamphlet that comes with it will have some recipes. The supermarkets are now featuring prepared and boxed ingredients for all types of slow cooker meals. I suspect their quality when compared to what you can easily do yourself but I suppose they will work when you are in a hurry or you are just plain lazy. In any event, you are going to love this method of cooking.

Crockpots and Dutch Ovens: If you have one you might want to give it a try. They are a lot like a slow cooker and the results can be great but don't buy one until you are a better cook.

Cooking a meal where everything comes out on time takes a little planning. Practice will improve this skill but to begin with think about what is going to take the most time to cook. It goes on first, obviously, but some things follow so rapidly that it is best to be ready to cook them before the first item goes on. For instance: fry bacon before you fry an egg. Put the toast in the toaster at the same time you fry the egg. Have the silverware, coffee, orange juice, salt and pepper, jam, and napkin out before you start any cooking. Breakfast cooks fast!

Manage meals the same way. You should be able to chop up a salad while the rest of the meal is cooking, but I wouldn't push it at first. Make the salad and wait to add the dressing. Potatoes can take longer to bake than most meat so get that in first. Mashed potatoes in the microwave are a three-minute item and they will hold. I like to heat canned veggies in a saucepan instead of in the microwave but that is just a personal preference. Heating more than one thing at a time in the microwave slows the process and doesn't do either item justice. Try both ways and see if you like the stove or the microwave. It's really your choice.

<u>Seasoning:</u> Don't clean out the spice rack at first. Unless you are into gourmet cooking, you are not going to need a lot of spices beyond salt, pepper, garlic powder, chili powder, Cajun sprinkle, Tobasco, basil leaves, cloves and cinnamon. Keep the pepper mill. Then you will want catsup, steak sauce, honey, and vinegar. All else is superfluous.

Season your food before or during the cooking. After all, that's what makes most food taste good. You may have to add a little extra seasoning at the table, but waiting until you are ready to eat before you sprinkle on the salt and pepper doesn't do the job. The seasoning is intense and therefore the flavor is more intense with the late addition.

11

A New Look at the Supermarket

Supermarkets today are a wonderland of temptations. As in the movie, Charlie and the Chocolate Factory, the stores are replete with sights and smells that will surely trap you into buying something that you did not plan. It's called impulse selling and you are the impulse buyer. Hardly a day goes by that you will not be seduced by a motherly type offering you a bite of some delicacy that is being featured. On a weekend you can literally eat your way through these sample offers without the need for making a purchase at all. It is dangerous to buy groceries when you are hungry. You will fall victim to merchandising unsurpassed in any other retail outlet.

It is a good idea to take a walk through your local supermarket without buying anything, just looking for what is available. Keep in mind what you are looking for are ways to make your cooking less of a hassle. The store is offering more and more ready prepared foods or foods that require very little preparation. Unfortunately, most of these items are in quantities too large for just one person and if it can't be cut in half or thirds it will be of little use to you unless you want to eat the same thing two or three times in a row. Here is what I discovered when I took a non-buying walk through my grocery store:

FROZEN FOODS—To begin with, you can buy a pretty good balanced meal in the frozen food department of any grocery store with the meal already prepared, seasoned and ready to eat. All that is required is to thaw the booger. You have three choices; the oven, the microwave, and the toaster oven. All will accomplish the task albeit within a different time frame. The package will provide you with the proper time and temperature, as well as any special instructions. These frozen dinners are good enough to carry you through the times when preparation or time frames are a hassle. The thing to remember about frozen prepared foods is that unless the quality is put into the product at the outset it will not be enhanced by freezing. Cheap is still cheap and most frozen dinners have been scrimped on in more ways than one to offer an attractive price. In this department you pay for quality.

Beyond frozen dinners you will find breakfast in the form of precooked bacon, sausage biscuits, breakfast burritos, waffles and pancakes ready for the toaster. Every kind of potato is available along with fruits, vegetables, breads and desserts.

For the pizza lover the frozen food department offers a great selection and you can find fresh ones as well. If you like pizza, I suggest that you purchase a ceramic plate for heating the pizza in your oven. They can be found in most department stores, kitchen stores and the like and when used it will help make that crust crispy once again. Also you will probably need to buy some crushed red pepper in the seasoning or spice department, if you don't already have it.

THE DELI DEPARTMENT—Here they cook the dish for you or it is already prepared and ready to eat. Chicken, brisket, ribs, sausage, burritos, potato salad, tuna salad, chicken salad, beans, Cole slaw, sliced cold cuts, pickles and soups make up the basic deli larder but there is plenty more. It is generally tasty, and can be purchased in any quantity required. The convenience comes with a higher price tag than what you can prepare for yourself but preparation time can be a factor if you have to put in a full day of work before you get home to fix your supper. It does provide some foods that are difficult to prepare for yourself. Potato salad and chicken salad is tough to prepare for just one or two servings, likewise for a few slices of brisket or some ribs. I like the deli for a fall back position to be used when time and the desire for someone else's cooking is called for.

Today most supermarkets have installed a salad bar which allows you to buy just the portion you want of such items as tuna or chicken salad, potato salad and hot soup. Rotisserie chickens are a good buy and provide enough meat for several meals. I remove all of the bones at the outset and store what I do not eat in a plastic container. Unless you prefer to spend a lot of time in the kitchen, you will find the delicatessen and frozen food section of your supermarket a true asset.

THE MEAT DEPARTMENT—Most everyone can fry or grill meat. Packaged meat is rarely presented in sizes small enough for just one person so "Ring the Bell". The butcher will cut or repackage an item in a size or quantity that you can handle. The beginning cook should stick with the simple items: pork chops, bacon, hamburger, steak, ham slices, hot dogs, and chicken parts. Don't buy a whole chicken. If you like white meat, buy a chicken breast. Other cuts like chicken thighs, wings, or drumsticks can all be purchased separately.

Before you refrigerate bacon, open the package and separate the slices, place them on a cookie sheet that is covered with waxed paper, then put the whole thing in the freezer. Once the bacon is frozen, stack it up, wrap a piece of waxed paper around it and put the whole thing in a plastic bag or empty bread bag and then store in the freezer. Then when you want bacon, you can remove just the amount you need and it's ready for frying. The same thing works for hamburger. You can buy a big amount of hamburger, bring it home, open the package and form the hamburger into tennis balls or patties, place on waxed paper, and freeze. Bag the meat in a freezer safe plastic zip-bag and you're ready for any number of hamburger recipes. Each tennis ball will make a quarter-pounder and, with any kind of rudimentary math skill, you should be able to apply this formula to any quantity called for by a recipe. I am unable to tell you why I prefer to store my hamburger in balls instead of patties. There is no best way.

This method of divide and freeze is useful for almost every multiple packaged meat, and it gives you the opportunity to buy in bulk or at least in packages that would normally be too big for a one person shopper. With a vacuum food saver, the frozen product can be packaged and stored for up to six months which should be plenty of time to eat up that package of rib eyes that was on special.

For now, roasts, ribs, fajitas, hams, and turkey can remain off the menu. There are plenty of ways to cook the basic items without attacking the more complicated ones.

THE DRY GROCERY DEPARTMENT—A walk through all of the aisles of the grocery department will yield plenty of ideas for the one-person shopper. Smaller cans of most products are available. Packages calling for the addition of hamburger can be cooked with limited experience. You might have to cut the contents in half to prevent having to eat the product for three consecutive meals, but a little extra seasoning and an extra dash of the real thing will help a lot.

Beef Stroganoff is a good example. A check of the ingredients on the box will tell you that sour cream is part of the powdered mixture that you will be adding to the hamburger meat. In addition to the boxed ingredients, add a tablespoon or two of the real thing and that fresh sour cream will pump up the flavor so the stuff is edible.

Check out the paper goods department and plan on adding some serviceable plates in a couple of sizes to your potential grocery list. I don't recommend plastic knives and forks but plates and even cups can cut down considerably on the dishwasher use. Don't plan to eat off of paper all of the time. It's depressing. Plan on having a nice relaxed meal at least once a week with a glass of wine, perhaps, and food presented on the good china.

THE PRODUCE DEPARTMENT—Don't overload on fresh vegetables or they will spoil before you get around to them. The hard vegetables will keep much longer than the soft ones. Produce departments over-water everything, knowing that you buy the water with the product. If you store it as wet as when you buy it, be prepared to lose a lot to spoilage. It may take a little time, but let the leafy stuff dry a bit and then wrap it in a damp paper towel before you refrigerate it. There are a number of packages of various mixes of leafy salad greens available. They are pretty big but they will keep long enough for you to prepare several salads before the package gets soggy. I find that a head of lettuce will keep crisp quite a bit longer if you keep the core attached.

A lot of produce today is presented in prepackaged form and is therefore too much for one person. Just ask the produce clerk to break up a package. You are not obligated to buy more than you want or need. Time will give you the experience to determine what quantities of fresh product to buy. After you throw out half of the tomatoes you bought last week along with the rotten bananas, you will learn to temper your purchases with the reality of your life style.

THE BAKERY DEPARTMENT—This is not a diet book nor is it designed to provide you with nutrition advice. You have to know what is good for you as opposed to what is just plain good and temper your shopping accordingly. So watch the pastries carefully. Nothing smells better than a bakery and nothing is better than fresh bread out of the oven with a mound of real butter on top. The same goes for doughnuts, cakes, cookies, crescent rolls, pies and the like.

Bread gets stale but not overnight. Pay attention to buy-by dates and buy the latest future date that is available. Bread, hamburger buns and hot dog buns come in packages for families not singles. If you are not a big bread eater, freeze half of the loaf. It won't taste like fresh after it's thawed and it will shrink a bit but it is edible. A light toasting will improve bread that has been frozen and thawed. If it seems too extravagant to buy six hamburger buns for one or two hamburgers then stop by the day-old bakery store. At least what you throw away won't cost you quite as much.

Purchase and then freeze a package of flour tortillas. Then thaw and freeze as needed to replace a slice of bread. You might find them a bit chewier but the convenience outweighs this and, as my daughter says, they make great wraps for hot dogs and you won't have to throw away four of the hot dog buns from a package of six.

SPECIALTY DEPARTMENTS—Supermarkets these days are filled with fish departments, sushi bars, gourmet aisles, hardware, housewares, liquor departments and more. Most of this stuff, except for an occasional fresh catfish or shrimp, might appeal, but will be of little need to you for quite a spell. We are providing the basics here. After you master the challenge of planning and cooking your own meals every day for six months, then you may be qualified to tune in

The Food Network or thumb through a recipe book. If you do watch the Food Network I have an unsolicited plug for you to watch "Paula's Home Cooking." Paula cooks with every artery clogging, calorie intensive ingredient that fashion models and dieticians abhor. Be prepared to gain a pound just watching her cook, but boy oh boy, it sure looks good!

I am not big on alcohol but I do like a glass of wine from time to time. The trouble is an occasional glass of wine is not conducive to a bottle of the stuff that will start to spoil as soon as it has been opened. I have solved the problem for me, at least. I buy my wine in a box. It may not be the best and it may be considered a sign of poor upbringing, but wine in a box doesn't spoil. The liner in which the wine is packaged collapses as it is used, thus keeping the remainder air tight and fresh. There is a problem with storage in the refrigerator because a box takes up quite a bit of space, but if you just drink red it won't require refrigeration anyway.

As a widower, you will spend more time in the grocery store than you ever did, even if you don't cook very much. Try to limit your visits and to buy only what you set out to purchase. Avoid impulse items if possible. A grocery list can be a big help but don't wait until you plan to go to the store to make one up. Keep a pad in the kitchen and when you recognize a need for an item, write it on your list. Otherwise you will find yourself running to the convenience store for something you forgot and paying extra for the convenience.

12

Stocking the Pantry

The most pressing question you will face each day, and you will face it each and every day, is what, when and where am I going to eat? This question is eternal and it will nag at you until the day you die. For a single male and, for that matter, any single individual, the answer gets more difficult with each passing day. It is why your wife or your mother used to ask you what you wanted for supper and let me tell you that the answer of, "I don't care," or "Anything will do" is not helpful, especially to someone who is tired of making that day by day decision.

Meal planning is not something you want to hear or read about so I will be brief. Ideally the organized, structured individual will sit down on Friday evening, plan his meals for the coming week, note what is needed in the way of supplies and shop for them on Saturday and prepare them on Sunday, put everything in containers for the refrigerator or freezer and finally adjust the halo over his head. I am not that organized or structured. Long term planning for me is sometime next week. Short term planning is almost immediate.

Meal planning, however short a term, will become a necessity or you will fall into the snacking trap which will result in obesity which could lead to diabetes and worse. A diet of Big Mac's and chicken wings won't cut it in the long term.

Most single men I have talked to who cook even a little make things in enough quantity to allow them to freeze it for the future. Stews, soups, chili, and some casseroles work well and can be made in sufficient quantity that they will provide several meals if stored and frozen in single serving containers and frozen. A quantity of packaged and sliced lunchmeats along with some assorted cheeses can make for a light lunch. I find that, because of spoilage problems, some frozen vegetables are a better buy than fresh ones because you can thaw out only what you want and the rest remains preserved for later use. The same is true for fruits such as peaches and berries.

Cooking for one person is a drag and the grocery stores are not very helpful for this category of consumer, but they are gradually at least providing a variety of quick prepared foods in quantities that you can divide into two, and sometimes more meals. If you don't get carried away with purchasing too many of these dishes at once, you will have a variety of meal choices available either frozen or in the package. Leftovers have a way of getting pushed back in the refrigerator and never retrieved until a layer of mold has been well established. You don't have to eat a leftover the next day but get rid of it, if it isn't frozen, within a few days.

I buy a lot of bulk meats when they are on special and separate them, seal in a food saver and freeze them. I always have some steaks, pork shops, ham steaks, chicken breasts, fish, and shrimp in individual serving sizes in my freezer. Frozen vegetables work best for me and I rarely buy beans, broccoli, or cauliflower fresh since I can thaw just the amount I might want and keep the rest. You can buy a medley of frozen vegetables for a stir-fry and only have to cook a handful instead of a host of fresh product, some of which is bound to spoil. You can even buy chopped bell pepper and onions in frozen packages. I use the chopped bell peppers but prefer to cut up my onions; although I do stock some frozen pearl onions which makes it easy to add onions to my slow cooker.

The slow cooker gets a workout around my house. It is so easy to cook with this appliance and it provides me with five or six individual servings of stew, soup, chili, roasts that I am never at a loss for something to eat. My freezer contains a variety of single serving meals that make it easy to eat a delicious and healthy meal without any more planning or cooking than to heat and serve.

I have a blender, that provides me with smoothies, which I also make in advance and freeze. Most of the ingredients for these smoothies consist of yogurt, banana, a frozen medley of fruit, a little Splenda and milk. You can buy smoothie mixes to use instead of milk and what you add is certainly up to you. Pour these mixtures in Styrofoam cups, snap on a lid and freeze. Keep one thawing in the refrigerator at all times. Add a sandwich or some cheese and pepperoni and you have a quick lunch that is both filling and effortless.

You just have to cook ahead in order to keep from being constantly faced with having to eat out or taking much more of your time than you want to feed that tapeworm. It is not necessary to prepare elaborate meals but it is in your best interest not to have to start planning supper at 6:30 p.m.

13

Boiling An Egg and Beyond

Cooking is a lot like freshmen chemistry. Weights and measures, heat and cold and time all combine to make a compound that is hopefully tasty and satisfying. Here are a few tips that will help you.

CLEANLINESS. Keep a clean kitchen. It is important to avoid poisoning yourself with otherwise healthful food. This means that you clean up before you cook, while you are cooking, and after your meal. Don't wait and don't fill up the sink with dirty pots and dishes. Aside from the odor the appearance of a dirty kitchen is not conducive to a good appetite nor is it a sign of discipline which is one of the basic human traits that must be developed when you find yourself living alone.

ORGANIZATION. Tune in to the Food Network and catch a show called Thirty-Minute Meals. No way does Rachel Ray, the hostess, cook a meal in thirty minutes without planning and organization. Her pots and pans are ready to go. The produce is all clean, fresh, and just out of the package. The pantry has all the items needed for that meal right up front and all of them are new for the first time. I'm not taking away from Rachel, who also fudges just a bit during commercial breaks, but it does point out that organization or a little planning will make things go easier and, more important, make everything come out on time.

The beginning cook should not try to do two or three things at once. Until you are comfortable with being able to prepare and toss your salad while frying chicken, do the short time work first. And that is the next clue. You must decide what part of your meal will take the longest to prepare and cook. If everything is to come out right, you have to time it so there is a chance for success.

When you are dealing with frozen items that must be thawed before you prepare them, it is best if you can let that item thaw naturally. To do this without leaving the product out on the counter all day, place it in the refrigerator the night before and it will thaw enough by the next day to be able to work with it. Thawing in the microwave is okay but don't just toss it in and flip the switch.

You will almost invariably overdo the thawing and enter into the cooking phase. Set your microwave to 50% and check the progress of the thawing.

INNOVATION. The beginning cook needs to follow the recipe or the cooking instructions on the box. Variations, except in seasoning, should be left for a time when you are more comfortable with adding something or taking something away from a recipe. Following the recipe means to follow it both in sequence and in the proper proportion. It is important to measure, especially when you will probably be cutting most recipes in half or thirds, or quarters.

LET'S COOK

So here we go. Remember, I have said earlier that this is not a diet book, nor is it nutritionally sound, nor is it a meal planner. All I can give you is some tried and true cooking methods and tips that have worked well for me. It will be up to you to go from there.

Canned, Boxed & Refrigerated Foods

CANNED VEGETABLES. Open a can and heat it. Gee, wasn't that simple? Well it's good to know that fixing a vegetable will be far from the most complicated item on your menu. Most canned vegetables are cooked in the can in a liquid that will taste pretty good if you just put it on the stove and heat it over a medium fire but a little seasoning will help a lot.

CORN. Corn comes in two basic varieties: whole kernel and creamed. Both are good. With whole kernel corn, I like to add a pat of butter along with salt and pepper while heating. You could add a little milk right at the end but that is up to your taste. You can serve whole kernel with or without the liquid it was canned in. Creamed corn is fine right out of the can. Add a little salt and pepper and you are off to the races. When I was a kid, creamed corn came with some corn in it. Now it is mostly gruel. If you have a package of whole kernel corn in the freezer or some leftover whole kernel corn, add it to the mix. It should turn that gruel into something a bit more substantial.

GREEN BEANS. Treat these the same as whole kernel corn, but this is an item that does well in the skillet as well as the saucepan. Jazzing up those beans in the skillet calls for a little extra work, but it is worth it. Have ready:

1 strip of bacon cut into small bits
3 slices of onion
In a skillet, fry the bacon in order to have bacon grease. Break up the onion slices

into slivers and add to the heated grease. Let sauté for a minute or two so that they will have a head start before adding the beans. Then drain the beans and add to the pan. Add a bit of salt and pepper and in three or four minutes you've got a great variation on what was just a can of beans.

P.S. You could also add some small mushrooms with the onions, but that may be way too gourmet.

OTHER BEANS. Baked, lima, kidney, black eyed, red, you name it. There is plenty of variety and, for the most part, all that is called for is to heat and serve. Add a hint of Tobacco and a pinch of salt, and you should be able to liven up what otherwise might be a bit bland, but some people like bland.

PEAS. By all means heat them in the liquid in which they were covered. After that you can drain them and serve them dry or keep the liquid and serve them in a bowl. I like to add milk to the liquid after the peas are heated. It doesn't take much, maybe two tablespoons, but it sure changes the flavor. A pat of butter and salt and pepper are always required.

ALL OF THE REST. Corn, beans and peas are the basics but there are plenty more as you well know and you can heat up whatever suits your fancy. I don't like canned asparagus but I love fresh. I like canned beets but wouldn't waste my time trying to cook them fresh. I know a person who makes his own sauerkraut but canned is fine for me. And so it goes. All you have to please is yourself and the dog or cat and they shouldn't be eating table scraps anyway.

STEWED TOMATOES. Here is another great heat and serve item, and I can't think of a thing to add except that I find that the tomatoes need to be cut up a bit smaller and you can do that while they are heating. Somewhere long ago I developed a taste for sweet with tomatoes. Everyone thinks I'm crazy but when I eat a fresh tomato I sprinkle a little sugar on it while everyone else adds salt and pepper. To that end I also add a bit of sugar to my stewed tomatoes. But that is a personal thing and I am probably the only person in the world who would desecrate a tomato in that manner.

POTATOES. You can buy a variety of potato flakes: some plain others with herbs, garlic or whatever. All are great for mashed potatoes and you can cook whatever quantity you want. The recipe is simple. Add a little water, some butter and milk, pop in the microwave and you have mashed potatoes in three minutes. Ain't technology grand!

Aside from potato flakes there are some new refrigerated packages of fresh potatoes that show a lot of promise. Included are potatoes with onions for hash browns and a couple more selections adding cheese and what-have-you. I tried the hashbrowns and they were great. The package is way too big for a one-person meal so I separated the package into three zip lock bags to prevent waste.

I suspect there will be more fresh refrigerated products coming down the line all the time so you need to look in the dairy and frozen foods sections. There is no telling what these retailers are cooking up to save the working wives time. Even the meat departments are getting in the act and you can now find brisket, ribs, stew, and all sorts of packaged meals that are not frozen and ready to heat and serve.

The problem still persists, however, that the packaging is not one serving friendly which means either that you must find a way of storing the rest or being prepared to eat the same thing several times over the next few days.

FRESH PRODUCE. Real men don't eat quiche and the same goes for salad except that, when offered one in a restaurant or given the opportunity with a buffet, then lettuce, tomato, onion, olives, and the kitchen sink appears on the plate, piled high with two or three tablespoons of the dressing of choice. I think the main objection most men have to the suggestion of a salad is that they don't envision a mound of lettuce as a meal all by itself. As an addition to a meal, the salad becomes more acceptable.

You are going to need to fix a salad more often than you think—about three times a week or more would be my guess if you are going to prepare a meal that you can sit down to and eat. That includes meals of the frozen or packaged variety. A fresh salad will enhance that meal and make the dining experience more pleasant.

Here are the basic salad ingredients that won't spoil too quickly:

Lettuce. The produce section now offers a variety of lettuce in bags and I recommend any one of them. It is by far the easiest way to build a salad and you can easily pick out a leaf or two when you want to have lettuce in your sandwich. If you must buy a head of lettuce, buy one that has some weight to it. The heavier the head the more densely packed are the leaves. My wife always removed the core from the head of lettuce when she prepared it for storage. I tried it that way to begin with but my lettuce spoiled too quickly. Obviously I don't eat as much lettuce as we used to so I changed my storage method. I now leave the core in the lettuce head, fold a dampened paper towel in the bottom of the crisper and place in the fridge. My lettuce lasts much longer this way. Leaving the ends of green onions on until needed and leaving the bottom intact on a stalk of celery are all good arguments for maintaining longer life of these produce items as well.

Tomatoes. Not every salad needs tomato nor does every sandwich but it won't hurt to keep at least one available. Whole tomatoes should not be refrigerated and once cut, tomatoes, even refrigerated have a short life. Buy small or cherry tomatoes so that when you do use them you will not be left with something that can dry out and spoil in a day.

Grocery store tomatoes have very little tomato taste and I have often wondered why some chemist who is good at creating artificial flavors for chips and things can't come up with a sprinkle that would enhance a tomato and bring it back to its home grown, vine ripened glory.

Onions. There is quite a variety here: white, yellow, and red. Far be it from me to recommend one over the other and frankly, if you are going to cook with them, I don't think it will matter. I like a sweet onion, especially in hamburgers, so I buy Videlia or an onion that is labeled sweet. Videlias come from some place in Georgia and unless they are from this section they cannot use the name Videlia. It's kind of like Bordeaux in France.

After the basic apple-sized onions you also have green onions (good for salads) shallots (I don't know anything about them), and pearl (little onions about the size of a walnut). My mother used to boil the pearl onions until they were tender and then cover them in a white sauce—delicious! I've got a recipe for these later in the book.

Keep some onions on hand. You will need them if you are going to do any cooking or frying. Store them dry and unrefrigerated in a container or bin that gets a little air circulation. They will last longer. By the way, refrigerate the green onions. I suggest you wet a paper towel and wrap the onions in that before placing in the fridge. You want them to remain crisp but not so wet that they rot.

Carrots. You can now buy carrots in small packages in finger sizes and even smaller. Keep a bag on hand. The big carrots are not good for much anymore but to shred and, if you watch your fingers, you can shred the finger size just as well. Store in the fridge; it might keep them fresher longer.

Bell Peppers. Another staple for salads, Pico de Gallo, and cooking is the bell pepper. They come in three colors: green, red and yellow. Green is the cheapest and frankly, unless you are in to color, red and yellow do not taste any better or any worse. Bell peppers mix well with hamburger meat and stews so they have more uses than just salads.

Potatoes. A tour of the grocery store will have shown you the availability of potatoes in nearly every section of the store. Potato flakes in boxes, french fries and scalloped in the frozen food section and fresh prepared in the dairy section. There are probably other potato varieties in the store but I haven't found them yet. It's hard to beat a baked potato and it is hard for me to obtain a well-cooked fluffy interior. A microwave will cook a potato but as I have already said, the interior will be "gummy." Most cookbooks say to bake a potato for one hour at 425 degrees. Mine take longer to cook and it may be because I live at 3,200 feet. The flesh is still not right. Incidentally, most restaurants can't seem to get a baked potato "right" either. It has been suggested that I preheat the potato in the microwave for a couple of minutes and then bake it in the oven. I have yet to try it but that might be a solution.

If you plan to cook a potato in the microwave, wrap it in plastic wrap and then stick a few holes in it with a toothpick. I left out the obvious. Clean the potato first with a brush unless you like a little dirt mixed in. This is essential if you plan to eat the skin along with the insides.

There are other varieties of potatoes beside the Idaho but for other than baked I suggest you buy them packaged not fresh. Sweet potatoes or yams will bake a lot faster for some reason and they can be cooked the same way as an Idaho potato. If you have eaten out lately you will have been offered a sweet potato as an alternative. Try one with a little honey butter and, if you like it, try one at home. The honey butter is easy. You can come close by mixing some soft butter with honey and ground cinnamon.

All other vegetables. Squash, zucchini, corn on the cob, green beans, eggplant, beets, rutabagas, jicama root, cucumbers, celery, radishes, okra, and whatever else I have forgotten, you can also forget, at least until you are a better cook than I think you are and your taste buds cry for the variety that these things can offer. If you want to know what to do with any of these things, look them up on the Food Network on your computer and, if you don't have a computer, learn to use one. It will help you while away the time, and, if you are newly single, you will have a lot of that on your hands.

Fruits. Apples, bananas, oranges, lemons, limes, and grapes all seem to develop a decent flavor in spite of being picked green and shipped thousands of miles. Peaches, plums, pears, strawberries, watermelon, cantaloupe, and pineapple are all iffy and must be sampled. The trouble is that most of these fruits are not fully ripened even when offered for sale and they must develop further at home. This piles on another problem: when the fruit ripens, it is likely to ripen all at once and must be eaten quickly or it is gone. The shelf life of an already ripe plum or pear is perilously close to none at all.

Stick to the basics but even in those cases, watch out when oranges are offered out of season. Today, fruit is imported so that it is available the year around but just remember, it ain't off the same tree. Australian oranges are not as sweet as the navels you are accustomed to, and grapes don't always come from California. I have found a great summertime treat you might want to try. When you buy grapes, take about half of the bunch, pull them from the cluster, spread them out on a cookie sheet and put them in the freezer. A handful of these frozen goodies make a great snack and they can be eaten right out of the freezer. No thawing is necessary because they don't get ice hard. If you have never done this, you will thank me for this one piece of advice if for none other.

The only fruit I know that remains consistent in flavor and texture wherever and whenever you buy it is the banana. How this jewel of a fruit can be raised largely in South America from a tree that produces a stalk twice a year, which is then harvested, cut into hands, boxed, taken to port, loaded on a ship, sailed to an American port, unloaded, trucked to a produce warehouse somewhere close to you, then gassed into almost ripeness, and shipped to the store all for a price that does not seem to reflect the labor, shipping and handling cost will remain a mystery. Count it a blessing and eat two or three a week.

Stick to the basics but even in those cases, watch out when oranges are offered out of season. Today, fruit is imported so that it is available the year around but just remember, it ain't off the same tree. Australian oranges are not as sweet as the navels you are accustomed to, and grapes don't always come from California. I have found a great summertime treat you might want to try. When you buy grapes, take about half of the bunch, pull them from the cluster, spread them out on a cookie sheet and put them in the freezer. A handful of these frozen goodies make a great snack and they can be eaten right out of the freezer. No thawing is necessary because they don't get ice hard. If you have never done this, you will thank me for this one piece of advice if for none other.

A farmers market is a great place to find good tasting fruit, tomatoes and the like. Be careful about buying produce that is not native to your area though. The farmers market is probably offering what cannot be raised from the same produce warehouse that your supermarket uses.

<u>Food Storage</u>. Keeping food from going stale or spoiling is a big problem for singles. Even foods that have been frozen have to be eaten within a reasonable period of time or they lose flavor or texture and while they may not spoil in the sense that they rot, they age to the point where they are no longer the food you wanted to save for later. When I first emptied the pantry I mentioned finding an old Seal A Meal and got rid of it as outmoded. I have since come full circle and have purchased an up graded model known as a Food Saver. Vacuum packing foods are, I have discovered, a great way to preserve foods for extended periods of time and that includes frozen foods.

It's a bit pricey out of the box but long range I think it will prove itself as an ideal aid in storage. Vacuum packing individual servings of frozen meats, fish and poultry will really make it worth while to buy these items in quantity because you can expect them to last at least a year without any loss of quality or condition. Another feature I like is the ability to vacuum things in Mason jars. I'm not sure how it works but you can chop up bell peppers, or onions or the like, place them mixed or individually in a Mason jar and suck the air out of the container. It will keep a pepper fresh and an onion from smelling up the fridge while all you have to do is pop the lid, pour out what you need for a salad or recipe and then reseal the jar.

As with any gadget, you can get carried away in using it but experience will temper with its application and it will be a great addition to your ziplock bags, plastic wrap, and plastic containers. Since acquiring my Food Saver I have sealed all of my current frozen meats and have resolved to eat my way through the food I now have in my freezer before buying another entree. It is a source of wonder to discover what all I have stored away with the idea of getting to it later on. I blame the fact that I have two refrigerators and a freezer and each refrigerator has a freezer compartment thus making it easy to accumulate much more than I truly should have in reserve. Murphy's Law applies here in that given the space you will find something to fill it. My grocery bill should go down for a while and maybe my electric bill will also be helped for I plan to turn off the freezer when I complete my mission.

I have noticed that my pantry is filling and shelf space is once again at a premium. A resolve here seems necessary as well. Just looking at the items I have in storage tells me that I am shopping without a list and, as a result, becoming a victim of impulse buying. You would think that having worked for a supermarket chain for 36 years, I would be immune but when I see three jars of peanut butter, two bottles of canola oil, an extra jar of mayonnaise, ketchup, jelly, and pickles, it tells me that, while I will probably use every bit of what is in that pantry, it would be much better if I let the supermaket store it at their expense and not at mine.

I will compliment myself a little bit about managing the contents of my refrigerator. I make a conscious effort to eat up what I have stored or set aside. If I open a can of corn and store half in a plastic container, I eat the remainder within the week. The same goes for most everything that qualifies as a leftover. I admit that I'm guilty of pulling out a container of pure mold from time to time, but it is rare and non of my guests have refused to eat, having examined my refrigerator.

14

What's for Supper?

Remember when you came home from work and asked that question? You will now appreciate why your wife did not give you an enthusiastic response to that query. I have said before but it is worth repeating: eating (when, where and what) is now one of your everyday concerns. I do not have the foggiest idea of your personal food tastes. You may be a lover of oysters, eggplant, brussel sprouts, and calamarie, all of which I will not eat unless served at a friend's house. Even then I will nibble my way through as small a serving as I can manage.

I feel compelled to share a few recipes of things that I like and find easy to prepare. Try these out if any of them sound like you might like them or delve through your wife's recipe collection. It should contain a lot of the dishes you have grown used to over the years.

STEW

I believe that if you do not now own a slow cooker, you should go out and buy one. They are not expensive and I would buy a large size while you can. A slow cooker stew is an ideal dish to make without any attention on your part once the ingredients are assembled. You can cook it just as well in a pot on the stove over low heat or even in a crockpot in the oven. The cooking on the stove will require more attention since it is not safe to leave a pot on a fire unattended. This stew can contain a variety of ingredients including the basic meat. While you can make stews with fish, chicken, lamb, beef and even vegetarian, my recipe is for beef stew. Other stews will follow the same procedure but the ingredients should change to reflect the meat being used. Where stated, the recipes I offer employ the use of a slow cooker. Cookers come in two sizes: three-quart and six quart. Buy the six-quart. It will allow you to increase the quantity of ingredients thus providing you with more meals to store in the freezer. Incidentally, you can purchase throw away liners for your slow cooker in the supermarket and they certainly make clean up of the cooker easy.

Beef Stew

Ingredients:

    1 lb. of stew meat
    1 pkg of small carrots
    1 or 2 potatoes cubed
    2 medium size onions, white or yellow
    1 or 2 green bell peppers cut bite size
    1 can diced tomatoes
    1 can Rotel tomatoes
    1 can or box of beef broth
    2 bay leaves
    1 jalapeno whole, not cut or chopped
    2 garlic pods
    1 tsp salt
    1 tsp pepper
    1 sprinkle pepper flakes or chili powder

Preparation:
Put stew meat in a plastic bag (I use bread sleeves that I save) with 1/4 cup of flour and shake well to cover all pieces.

In a skillet add canola oil and lightly brown stew meat. Do not overcook.

Place browned stew meat in the crockpot along with all of the other ingredients. Add water or more beef broth if stew looks like it needs more liquid.

Set slow cooker for six to eight hours on low and forget it. Cut cooking time in half if cooking on high.

If you are concerned about how spicy hot the stew is, you can cut back on the jalapeno, or peppers and count on spiking the stew with hot sauce when you are ready to eat it.

You may add other vegetables to the list above but don't overdo it. Corn, celery, green beans, or zucchini will work but they will get pretty soft and not add much flavor.

When the stew is done, fish out the bay leaves, garlic pods and whole jalepeno before serving then ladle up a bowl full for supper and put the remaining stew in individual serving containers and freeze. It should make about five to six servings.

Once you have made a stew in your slow cooker, you can see the possibility for variety with this cooking appliance and the beauty is that cooking is a breeze and the product is mistake proof.

Pot Roast

The slow cooker will prepare a roast to perfection and it doesn't matter what kind of meat you select. Chuck, arm, rib, round, top sirloin—all will do nicely.

Ingredients:

- 2-4 lb. roast
- 2 medium-sized onions cut in chunks
- 1 handful of small carrots
- 1 or 2 medium size potatoes quartered
- 1 tbs. Kitchen Bouquet
- Salt and pepper
- 1/2 can of beef broth (optional but I think moisture is needed)

Preparation:

Rub the roast with Kitchen Bouquet and place in cooker. In lieu of Kitchen Bouquet you can brown the meat in a skillet before placing in the cooker. Add other ingredients, set the cooker for six to eight hours on low, put on the lid and forget it. Resist the urge to lift the lid during cooking to check on the progress. When cooking on low, the heat loss resulting from lifting the lid reduces the temperature and slows the cooking time. You can cook the roast dry but I like to add a little broth. This broth can be used as a sauce for the roast. By the way, don't trim the fat before you cook the roast. It will add both moisture and taste to the dish. Some people who are wild about garlic pierce the roast in several places and insert cloves of garlic for added flavor. For a different taste pour a package of Lipton's Onion Soup Mix on top of the roast and to cook it up even another notch add a can of can of condensed cream of celery soup.

Green Chili Stew

Here is a wonderful recipe that might not take regular chili out of your life but this one will add an additional warm and hearty meal that is easily prepared in your slow cooker.

Ingredients:

- 2 lbs lean pork cubed
- 1/4 cup flour

1 tsp cumin
1/4 tsp pepper
1 tsp salt
1 tsp ground sage
3 tbs oil
3 tbs vinegar
2 large onions coarsely chopped
2 cans small whole or cubed new potatoes, drained. Can use fresh if you prefer.

2 or 3 green chilies diced or 1 can (4 oz) More won't hurt
2 cups tomatillo salsa (salsa verde) Use green chili salsa if you can find it.
1 can chicken broth. More if you want stew to have more liquid.
1 tsp brown sugar

Preparation:

Place flour, cumin, pepper, salt and sage in a plastic bag, add pork cubes and shake to cover meat thoroughly. Brown pork in hot oil in batches place in slow cooker. With heat still on, add vinegar to the skillet (keep your head back) and scrape up the brown bits in the pan. Place all of the rest of the ingredients in the cooker along with the scraped bits. Stir, cover and cook for 8 to 12 hours on low. You can mash a few of the potatoes if you want a thicker stew.

Slow Cooker recipes abound. A lot will come with the cooker itself. Variations are available on the Internet in any number of sites. I use the Food Network site to begin with, but absent any site you can. Just search for the recipe by the name of the dish. I would add "slow cooker" to the dish for which I was searching.

Soups

When you are desperate for a fast lunch, a can of tomato or chicken noodle soup will often do the trick. But if you have the time you can easily make some soups that are worth making in quantity and freezing in individual serving containers. Here are a couple of my favorites:

Mexican Cheese Soup

This soup is a mess to make and it is time consuming. I wouldn't make it at all but it is so darn good that when I have the time and the inclination, I set out to produce a big pot—enough to last me for quite a while. It is another good item to keep available in the freezer. My children all seem to look forward to a serving when they come to visit.

Ingredients Stage One:

- 3 tbs margarine
- 2 cups of carrots shredded
- 1 can of diced green chilies
- 1 jalapeno pepper finely chopped
- 2 cups of onion finely chopped
- 2 cups of green bell pepper finely chopped
- 1/2 cup all purpose flour

Preparation Stage One:

Sauté vegetables in margarine until soft. Add flour and stir to mix well. Remove from heat and set aside.

Ingredients Stage Two

- 6 tbs flour
- 4 cups of water
- 1 1/2 cups of chicken broth (if you want more chicken broth reduce the amount of water proportionately)
- 1 stick of butter (not margarine)
- 3 cups to 1 qt heavy cream
- 4 cups grated cheddar cheese
- 4 cups grated pepper jack cheese

Preparation Stage Two:

Make a roux (paste) by melting butter in a large saucepan and add flour, stirring over low heat. When fully incorporated, add the cream and water and heat slowly. Pour this cream mixture into a pot large enough to accept the vegetables and cheese. I use a turkey broiler. Add cheese to hot cream mixture. Stir constantly until cheese melts and mixture is smooth. Add vegetable mixture and stir well on low heat.

I go heavy on the cheese in this recipe and you can cut back if you desire, but frankly, the more cheese the better. The diced green chilies won't add much spice heat but the jalapeno may. Cut back on the amount of jalapeno if you are afraid it might get too hot.

On any foods you cook, unless you plan to freeze them, you should try to cook or prepare only what you plan to eat at that time. That is not always possible since some things cannot be cut back to one serving, but where you can, prepare meals to avoid leftovers. That is, of course, unless you want to eat that meal again within a very few days.

Keep some frozen dinners on hand. Sandwich makings should be available from your refrigerator. Deli ham, chicken, turkey, pastrami, bologna, salami, and hot dogs are all available in packages small enough for you to store one or two of your favorites. A package of American cheese slices will keep forever and with these items available, a good sandwich, fresh or grilled is only minutes away.

If what you plan to eat the next day calls for thawing, get it out of he freezer the night before and store it in the refrigerator. It should thaw partially by morning and be ready for you whenever you want to cook it. Cooking frozen meats is not a good idea unless you are going to bake them slowly in the oven. Instant heat will not thaw meat evenly and you will most assuredly ruin a good steak if you throw a frozen sirloin on a hot grill. You can thaw meat in a microwave but be careful that you do not start cooking it. Choose a thaw setting along with a short period of time. It is better to thaw slowly, else you will start to cook the meat and that cannot be a good thing.

A blender can be a big help in adding fruit to your diet. A cup of yogurt (any kind will do), a cup of frozen fruit (I buy the frozen medley), some sugar or sweetener to taste, and a quantity (your choice) of either milk, cream, or ice cream and you have a great smoothie which can be used for a snack or breakfast. Add a quarter cup of grape nuts and you will get a little crunch. Obviously, other ingredients besides yogurt and milk can be used with fruit and the combinations can be endless. Smoothie liquids are available in the supermarket and you can add your own ingredients to beef up the store-bought stuff.

You don't have to have a sandwich grill to grill a good ham and cheese sandwich or any sandwich, for that matter. If you like grilled sandwiches and don't have a suitable grill in your kitchen, you can use a regular frying pan as your grill. Just make up your sandwich for grilling, lightly butter one side and place into a hot frying pan (non-stick required). Press the sandwich down with a spatula then quickly butter the top half of the sandwich while it is still in the pan. Turn the sandwich over and toast the other side. Add a few chips and a pickle to your plate and voila, lunch!

You are what you eat and living a single life can lead to way too much starch and not enough vegetables and fruits. You can buy a container of carrot and celery sticks packed in water and, if you change the water frequently, they will keep well in the refrigerator for longer than the packaged variety. Put out a piece or two with your sandwich or dinner. You can heat a can of beans, corn, or peas without any trouble or time. Make two or three thick slices of tomato and, while you are grilling your meat or in a separate pan, grill the tomatoes with a sprinkle of shredded cheese on the top. Mushrooms are another good quickie cooked in a pan with a little oil. Add a slice or two of onion roughly chopped and, if desired, a dash of wine.

When I tire of cooking vegetables, a can of V-8 juice does a pretty good job of a down and dirty substitute. I do the same thing for a fruit fix except I make smoothies that I have discussed earlier.

The peanut butter sandwich returns to the widower's palate as an easy snack or lunch staple. I make a peanut butter sandwich that few have ever tried. I toast it in a toaster oven. I know about peanut butter and banana sandwiches and peanut butter and jelly but toasting adds a different flavor to the peanut butter. You can butter one side of the bread and this seems to enhance the whole thing. Another different peanut butter sandwich that offers a unique taste is to add salad dressing to one side of the sandwich. I can't describe the flavor but if you like salad dressing give this one a try.

I am not big on pasta but I have one casserole type dish that is easy to make and stores well frozen. It calls for one pound of hamburger, one 10+-ounce can of Franco American Spaghetti, and a bell pepper. In a large frying pan cook the hamburger until well done but not burned. While cooking the hamburger, break it into small bits with the spatula. When the hamburger is done and crumbled, drain off the grease through a colander. Place back in the pan and add the spaghetti along with at least half of a bell pepper that has been chopped. Mix thoroughly while the mixture is heating. Add Parmesan cheese, salt and pepper to taste and it's ready. Garlic toast would compliment this dish greatly but it is not essential. Freeze half of it for later.

I have a friend in Germany who worked long enough in the United States to become hooked on Mexican food—the hotter the better. Every six weeks or so I send him a small box of jalapeno peppers for a pepper fix. He can get most of the other ingredients locally but fresh jalapenos are unheard of in Hamburg.

I am not the pepper belly that my friend is but I do love Mexican food or at least my version of it. Here is one of my favorites:

Pico de Gallo

This is really a basic that can be used as a side dish or added to other ingredients for a great and colorful main dish. You can buy it fresh in any quantity at the salad bar of your supermarket. It does not keep well but you can hold some of it overnight in the fridge. Beyond that, throw it out.

Chop up a tomato, half a bell pepper, and half of an onion. Before chopping up the tomato, cut it in half and squeeze out most of the juice. The pico should not be watery.

Add to the mix a fresh jalapeno chopped fine. Here the amount of pepper is up to you. Start with the lower half including whatever seeds are there. The seeds and the white inner veins contain most of the heat and I would add these seeds slowly and cut the liner out. This stuff will get on your hands so wash them well before you proceed. You don't want to rub your eyes with the oil from the jalapeno on your fingers—you will do this only once.

Chop up some fresh cilantro. This is a leafy plant like parsley. Some will tell you that you can leave this out but the taste of your pico will suffer greatly without it. About a fourth of a cup will do. It won't keep long in the fridge but it is cheap so be prepared to waste most of what you buy.

Add garlic salt, and pepper to taste and let it meld in the refrigerator until needed.

A great supper item can be made using the Pico de Gallo you have made and this is one of my favorites and easy to prepare.

You will need A tostada—6 or 8 inch

> Refried beans
> Shredded cheddar or jack cheese
> The pico

A tostada is a round corn tortilla fried crisp. You can buy these in the store or you can fry one in a skillet from a regular corn tortilla. Purchased, they come in a box and will keep as long as your chips—longer if you freeze them.

Now, smear on the refried beans. You can skip these if you are on a low carb diet and the thickness of this paste is up to you. I like about 3/8th's of an inch. (Can you imagine putting that measurement in a recipe?) On top of the beans add pico evenly over the pie and top it off with a healthy amount of shredded cheese. Pop it into the microwave for however long it takes to melt the cheese (about two minutes) and you have a meal that will compliment that margarita you fixed ahead of time. Note also, that in addition to tasting great, being easy to prepare and making very little mess, it really looks good. What other food comes with a mix of red, green, and yellow?

I find Chinese food better served in a restaurant but that is probably because I live in West Texas where the possibility for Chinese take out is not very prevalent. I can offer no ideas for fast and easy meals that are strictly ethnic in nature, since what I cook for myself is my own mixture of meats, vegetables and seasonings. You will develop your own favorites and your own cooking style as your single life goes on. I hope you get better at it up to the time when, due to your age or infirmity, you will have to move to a retirement home or welcome the visits of Meals on Wheels.

PART IV
Making Adjustments

15

Teaching Time To Fly

They say that it is essential to remain active in order to maintain your health both physically and mentally. This is especially true for the widower who is no longer employed or being still employed finds himself with less demand on his time when he gets home. Household duties will call upon some of your time but by no means will you be inclined to spend all of it in household chores. The same is true for evening entertainment. While you might go out on the town once or twice a week, you will find plenty of extra hours on your hands that will drag you into a lounge chair in front of television and another couch potato will be born.

Physical activity should be part of your regimen. If by now you don't already have some exercise program, it is time to start one. There is any number of physical fitness enterprises available, provided you can't stand to exercise by yourself. Treadmills, rowing machines, stair steps, weights, running tracks, all are available at these locations but they are equally available for home use. Garage sales are loaded with good buys of exercise equipment that for whatever reason has been set aside. Personally, I recommend a less strenuous approach. At my age, a round of golf, a walk with the dog, and an occasional bicycle ride around the neighborhood keep all of my joints moving without protest.

For most of my working life, I functioned as Director of Human Resources and Labor Relations for a supermarket chain that operated in Texas, New Mexico, Colorado, and Arizona. It is now bankrupt which is another book that will not be written. Most of my duties dealt with labor relations. This is a thankless job that satisfies neither management nor labor but I enjoyed the give and take this work entailed. I retired before the government made it almost impossible to hire, fire, promote or demote workers without a paper trail a mile long and a work place filled with split toilet seats, hand rails, helmets, and safety regulations out the kazoo.

I have always depended heavily upon some form of mental and physical activity as a hobby. Through the years I have taken on several arts and crafts activities to keep me occupied. For most of my life I have maintained an interest in drawing. I am not a talented artist. I cannot draw figures well, but I can, after many years, manage a pretty good landscape or still life. This started in school and then became a form of doodling while sitting in long drawn-out labor negotiations.

I became acquainted with a fellow employee whose hobby was watercolor painting and he introduced me to the medium. I had tried painting in oils and acrylics but found them to be slow and messy. Watercolor, on the other hand, can be fast and clean and it is done in the same way that you draw, which is to draw or paint in the dark places and leave the light areas to show up.

Drawing is a good hobby. You can do it almost anywhere as long as you have a pencil and piece of paper. There are not many hobbies you can carry around with you that easily. Even without paper and pencil you can plan a drawing or painting mentally because each picture is a series of steps and when you paint with watercolor you need to work fast before the paint dries.

A hobby is not a profession and I resisted any efforts to make it even a minor one. I rejected all requests to paint someone's old home place, or water tank or windmill. While I am capable of doing a satisfactory job of such an assignment, to do so would turn what is an enjoyable pastime into a labor. Painting and drawing is a hobby I continue but not as actively as I once did.

I believe in hobbies or crafts because they provide an opportunity to work with your body and your brain. Gardening, leather tooling, carving, ceramics, mechanics, carpentry, bicycling, golf, tennis, swimming, dancing, singing, playing an instrument—are all activities which will keep you both physically and mentally active.

If you have yet to join the twenty-first century by all means do so and at the very least, buy a computer. They are inexpensive and the learning curve is pretty low. Your children can fix you up in a few minutes or you can take a class at a senior citizens' center or at your local college. Once you start sending and receiving e-mail, you will be hooked. It's a great way to stay in touch with your children and your friends and, while it may not be as good as a telephone conversation, you will soon find that you are anticipating checking your email every morning. Your computer can provide hours of entertainment and, just like watching television, you can bury yourself in front of the screen. For all of that, I find it to be a wonderful invention with countless opportunities to access the wonders of this world as well as interact with people everywhere.

Not only is it necessary to develop activities, it is also vital that you get back in circulation. I don't mean entering into the dating scene. That might come to some in time but at the beginning you must find ways and means to be with people—at your church, your hobby club, your sport event (active or spectator) or by volunteering for any number of activities. Stay-at-home moms in my day used to complain that they needed adult companionship and interaction. Bringing up a baby and watching soaps all day is not conducive to mental stimulation. We all need to talk, to gossip, to laugh, to listen with other people.

Every city, town and hamlet now has a senior citizens center. It is a place to start. You will find that the longer it has been since your spouse's death, the less interest your married friends will have in including you in their activities. It is not because they are indifferent to your plight but you just don't fit in as a single. Before long you will need to seek out a companion who will once again provide that opportunity to be socially acceptable among married couples.

I want to get out in the world more than I do now. It is not that I am not occupied but I can sense that I need more interaction. Right now I play golf three times a week, weather permitting, I serve on the Civil Service Commission (a once a month job), the Science Spectrum board (little work but good conversation) and attend church, prayer breakfast, and Sunday School. I eat out at least once a week with friends and I have taken up decorating gourds. It's not enough. I have registered with the Life Long Learning Center at our university and plan attending some lectures, plays, and a trip or two. There is still a lot of time left. Too much for me.

Fairly early in my career as a widower I signed up for and was taking assignments as a substitute teacher for junior high and high school students. The work opportunities were unpredictable but frequent enough for me. I didn't do this for the money but for the experience of being with young people once again and maybe helping just a little. What an eye opener! I quickly learned that the school of my youth no longer existed. Subs are raw meat for the animals that we have caged up in the public school system. It wouldn't be so bad if they gave you a whip and a chair the way Frank Buck was equipped when he entered the lion cage of the old Barnum and Bailey Circus. Today's substitute teacher is naked with only one threat of a report to the principal as their ineffectual weapon. No striking, no touching, no threats, no back up, and rarely a workable class assignment from the absent teacher. The students know it and they take full advantage of your weaknesses.

It is frustrating and very stressful. You would expect, at least I did, that thirteen and fourteen-year-olds would show some respect for a man who is probably older than their grandfather. Don't believe it. "May I be excused to go to the bathroom," is the first test of each new class period. Then all it takes is for the class clown, and there always is at least one, to set the tone for the day and the chaos begins. Assignments are ignored, "Mr." and "Sir" are not in the vocabulary and the day deteriorates from period to period. I stand in awe of any person, who elects the teaching profession, as I am in awe that achievement tests are reported with any result of a passing grade. Where do they learn enough to pass a test? It is not in the schools where I substituted. While I may feel the need for outside contact, life is too short to volunteer for the aggravation of intermingling with the youth of this generation. Oh I know there are good kids out there; my grandchildren are good kids aren't they? At least at home they are. But in school, who knows?

As I have said a little earlier, a lot of what you did as a couple is no longer open to you. No one needs a regular single for bridge club or dominoes. If you were in a dance club you might be able to hang in there but only because our generation approved of stags and welcomed variety in dance partners. But you can volunteer for activities that will offer you opportunities to interact with people. Almost any hospital will take you in a variety of capacities. Your church has a number of opportunities that you can accept in visiting capacities or serving as a receptionist, bookkeeper, and even custodian. If you have the stamina, supermarkets would welcome you in a variety of jobs. I have one reservation on which there is no compromise and it prevents me from accepting many job opportunities. I want my freedom and interaction too. It is selfish, I know, and it will make volunteering for any regular type of activity pretty difficult. Volunteers are needed and welcome in all sorts of activities and if you are so inclined you can help yourself and the agency you serve as well. A word of caution, however. Your generosity can be abused and you will find yourself working more than you planned.

I have a mixed emotion when the word volunteer is used. Any ex-serviceman will tell you, "Do Not Volunteer." Nothing good ever seemed to come from a call for volunteers. Knowing that, my drill instructor in boot camp once called for volunteers for a special assignment to step forward. Only four or five people stepped forward wherein the drill instructor let the five off duty and volunteered the rest of us for the detail. This proves my point. Nothing ever good comes from volunteering.

If you don't need the money and you have the time, you are a valuable asset provided you are willing to work for nothing. With that offer going for you, look for something to do that you really think you will enjoy. Audit a class at the local university or college. Get associated with Habitat for Humanity, and my best idea yet: set yourself up as a handyman for widows who need odd jobs done that they cannot perform themselves. Word of your availability will spread like wildfire and the work can sometimes be more rewarding than just helping a damsel in distress.

16

Is There Anyone Up There?

I am a member of the Methodist Church. I cannot honestly say that I am a Methodist. I believe that our universe and everything in it was created by a superior entity that I call God and I am able to reconcile the findings and speculations of science as His proof. At this point, if you cannot accept at least this much of theology, skip this chapter.

My wife was a Christian and it troubled and vexed her a great deal that I could not accept her belief as fully as she would have liked. She didn't push me and we did not argue about our respective beliefs. Her death has changed my thinking to some degree. Like everyone else that I know, I hope for a heaven, a place more perfect than this earth which I see as full of errors that heaven is to correct. I want to believe that there is consciousness of some kind after death and that is where my wife is. Her heaven is different than mine and it gives me comfort to believe that she is in her heaven and will visit me in mine after I am gone. I think everyone's idea of life after death or heaven is unique.. It's no longer just streets paved with gold and angels with harps singing in the clouds. You are free to pick your own little spot of perfection. For now, at least, you can be a creator. Build it how you want. Wipe out sickness, get rid of bodies, play golf all day, eliminate sleep, travel the universe, visit with Socrates or Elvis. You are only limited by your imagination.

I do not apologize for believing in an existence after death. Every civilization and tribe before me have had their own beliefs on this subject, even as far back as the Neanderthal. It is the universal wish and it sustains us all. Churches don't preach much about heaven anymore. Preachers when I was a kid scared me about it and, based on their requirements for admittance, I was pretty sure I wasn't going to get in. That is the start of where my wife and I found different beliefs. While I believe that there are universal social laws about murder and stealing, we differed on what it was going to take to be accepted.

But church and church attendance are different from belief. I value my church membership a great deal. The funeral service for my wife was truly a celebration of her life. The ministers are sincere in all that they do and I find that I enjoy attending church services now more than I did in the past. It was hard at first to go back to church because my wife enjoyed it so much. I made myself sit in the same general area where we always sat. During those first months I couldn't sing the hymns without choking up in the middle of the first verse. I'm not certain what caused that but I am convinced that I am closer to my wife when I am in church than at any other time. I can almost feel her giving me a nudge to make certain I am awake, for, you see, I like to close my eyes when I listen to a speaker. There is less distraction and I can concentrate on what is being said. My wife never understood that and believed I was trying to go to sleep, so when I closed my eyes I would hold her hand and squeeze it from time to time to reassure her that I was awake and paying attention. I can now sing a hymn without getting all teary eyed and choked but I still miss my wife the most when I am in church because I am closer to her there.

We attended Sunday school even more religiously than church but for the last ten years; at least, we were members of separate and unique classes. My wife's class was made up of women only who were in their sixties and above—a mixture of widows and wives. Right next door were the husbands and widowers of that same group. There might have been a few who didn't fit that mold but it is a pretty good description of the two classes. How these classes got started I do not know but I suspect the women agreed to the separation because they were tired of looking after us and they wanted a group of their peers without those dirty old men. The men are just as happy and I suspect that the lessons taught in each class, even if by the same teacher, would be presented in an entirely different way.

Given a sickness, a crisis of some kind, or a death, and both groups will marshal their forces to help the afflicted party. As in any church, a member who is suffering for whatever reason can expect love and support. Your church friends are a fountain of help when you need it the most. In addition, people who have a religious faith of any kind will give you strength by the very fact that their belief strengthens them and it is clearly visible. One of my sisters claimed to be an atheist but a kinder, more generous person you could not find. Church going doesn't have a lock on compassion but it is where to go when you find yourself alone.

Church doesn't require membership. You will be welcome and you can participate. It is also a wonderful place to make use of some of the time you find on your hands. If you attend church regularly there are always calls for volunteers to act as usher, greeter, communion server, choir singer, scripture reader, teacher, clerk, or hospital visitor. Depending on the size of the church, there could be other duties for which you could volunteer. I attended Preston Wood Baptist Church in Plano, Texas, with my son and his family. Preston Wood is a megachurch with thousands of members and every amenity you could imagine. It is obvious that they make use of volunteers for all kinds of things that I would not have dreamed would be needed. From trombone players to parking attendants to traffic directors, the church is a beehive of volunteers behind the scenes. Such a church is not for me. I need the closeness I feel with my Sunday school class and the warmth I enjoy from a church service that is a little less of a production.

I suppose that, on reflection, my wife's death has strengthened my beliefs and although they are a long way from what my wife would have me believe, they are more solidified and clear to me now than ever before. I would not impose my religious beliefs on anyone. In a church atmosphere I qualify as a skeptic, for I must struggle with my acceptance of science and guard against any wishful thinking on my part. Science does not have all of the answers and I am left at least with the wonder that my DNA does not contain my awareness of self or my ability to remember. To me, these are God given. That God has bestowed upon me these unique characteristics proves to me that there is more to our lives on this spec of dust than happenstance and that we are challenged to seek its purpose. It is an unconventional testimony and yet one which has been accepted on occasion by the members of my Sunday School class where I substitute as a moderator from time to time. I am comfortable teaching this group because they love me as I love them and they accept me for what I am and isn't that what we are called to do?

17

Tomorrow and Tomorrow and Tomorrow

A lot of things have changed since I have become a widower. I have had an opportunity to reflect more about things that I had previously set aside for later in life. Well, it is now later in life and my new status has caused me to re-evaluate some of the things that had not been a part of my life plan prior to my wife's death. There are some plusses in my new status but they don't offset the minuses. It's like the offer, "I have some good news and some bad news. Which do you want to hear first?" Let's discuss the bad news first.

After years and years of cooperative living, you are now required to do this without a companion. The tug-of-war that defines most marriages is gone. Regardless of new friendships or even new companions, the life you lived previously cannot be shared. You will miss that terribly. It is the grief that will remain with you always.

Living alone will not be easy. That's what this book is supposed to help you accomplish The mundane chores of getting through each day, cooking and cleaning and fixing present challenges that were not anticipated or welcomed. Moving into assisted living, while sometimes necessary, just substitutes one set of problems for another.

What to do with time is a big question. Just a while back there never seemed to be enough time. Now, demands on your time no longer exist in the manner to which you had become accustomed. It is ironic that having been freed from the requirements of living as a couple you now find yourself missing those very impositions.

You will lose a lot of friends. Things you did as a couple will no longer be available to you. A companion will help you regain a couple status but a lot of couple friends will change.

What about the good news? Is there any good news? Not really. You will enjoy, sometimes, a sense of freedom from responsibility, a thing you have lived with all of your married life. You are able to do some things now that you would never have done when you were married. I don't mean the sinful things, although I suppose there is that possibility. I mean you can go to action movies if that is your desire. You can play 27 holes of golf instead of 18. Vacation at the beach instead of the mountains or vice versa. You can lounge in a recliner and watch Monday Night Football. You can even smoke a cigar in the house but responsibility will not disappear, you will still need to mow the lawn, water the plants and feed the dog. Even those new found freedoms will lose their fascination. After all, where is the joy in doing something to which there is no objection?

This is not to say that you should not nourish your zest for life. Maintain your curiosity. Keep alive those things that have given you joy, friendships, music, sports, reading, hobbies, religion, travel, and all of the activities that serve to enhance and enrich your life. Keep your memories for they will sustain you, but do not dwell on the past. You still have an obligation to live your life to the fullest. Do this not only for your own physical and mental well being but also for your friends and family who will be relieved by your adjustment and comforted in the knowledge that a person they love is doing okay.

I am now a widower and I am learning to adapt to this life. It is not the life I would have chosen and it is not a life I would wish on anyone else but death will separate all of us for a time. It is my fervent wish that those of you who have joined me in this stage of life will grieve over your loss, adapt to your new status and move on.

The End

About the Author

Bob Hurmence is a retired widower who found himself suddenly single. Having worked thirty-five years in the corporate world as Vice President and Director of Human Resources for a West Texas Supermarket chain he then purchased and operated a commercial printing business for the last ten years of his working life. Retirement followed with the promise of a life together filled with travel, golf, grandchildren, leisure, hobbies and good food.

A veteran of WWII. He assembled a collection of service memories furnished by prominent citizens of Lubbock, Texas. Titled, "A War Remembered," the book became popular enough to sell out of its limited printing. Hurmence holds a BBA and MBA from Texas Tech University with graduate work toward a PhD at New York University. Nothing outside of the sudden and unexpected death of his wife Boots qualifies him as an expert widower with the exception that he is living as one and is compelled to share the experience.

978-0-595-44254-6
0-595-44254-4

Made in the USA
Middletown, DE
05 June 2024